LOOKIN

Former Pennsylvania Governor Mark Schweiker:

Just 10 months after the horror of 9-11, my work as Governor of Pennsylvania brought me back to Somerset County to launch what seemed like to many a hopeless rescue effort of nine coal miners trapped in the Quecreek Mine well below Bill Arnold's farm. Through his moving account of how the citizens of the local community, commonwealth, nation and the miners' families came together to inspire our effort, Bill's story puts the reader alongside our remarkable rescue team as we worked feverishly and prayerfully with every tool we had to reach them alive. Looking back, we experienced much more than a successful rescue; we encountered the mighty hand of divine providence guiding us to an outcome that observers now call the "miracle at Quecreek".

David E. Hess, Secretary of the Pennsylvania Department of Environmental Protection, at the time of the rescue:

I cannot say enough about how proud I am of the job the men and women of the Department of Environmental Protection did to bring about the safe rescue of the nine miners at Quecreek. From those in Deep Mine Safety handling the details of the rescue itself, to the water quality staff dealing with the millions of gallons of water being pumped out of the mine, our communications staff who worked around the clock with the unprecedented world-wide media attention and even our summer interns on-site who got the experience of a lifetime.

Hundreds of people from DEP and other state agencies were involved, working along with our federal counterparts and the entire Somerset community, to achieve a single goal, knowing, the entire time, the odds were not on our side. This is the story of how we all converged on Bill Arnold's farm, and over four very long days 15 years ago, were witness to what I can only call a miracle.

MIRACLE
AT
QUECREEK
MINE

Blessings!
8-19-23

MIRACLE
AT
QUECREEK
MINE

By
Bill Arnold

Bill Arnold

ENCOURAGE
PUBLISHING

Miracle at Quecreek Mine

Copyright © 2017 by William R. Arnold. All rights reserved.
No part of this publication may be reproduced, stored in a retrieval system or transmitted in any way by any means, electronic, mechanical, photocopy, recording or otherwise without the prior permission of the author except as provided by USA copyright law.

Printed in Canada

Library of Congress Control Number 2017948785
Cataloguing data:
William R. Arnold
Miracle at Quecreek Mine
ISBN 978-0-9985592-4-7 (paperback ed.)

1. CHRISTIAN LIFE / Stories
2. CHRISTIAN LIFE/Miracles
3. HISTORY / United States/State and Local/Mid-Atlantic
4. PENNSYLVANIA/Description and Travel

The opinions expressed by the authors are not necessarily those of the publisher.

Published by Encourage Publishing, *LLC*
New Albany, Indiana 47150 USA
1-812-987-6148
info@encouragebooks.com
www.encouragebooks.com

Book design and layout by Encourage Publishing, LLC. All rights reserved.
Cover design by Leslie Turner
Cover photos courtesy of Bill Arnold and licensed through ShutterStock
Interior design by Ahaa! Design + Production
Editing by Leslie Turner

DEDICATION

This book is dedicated to all the rescue workers,
from the most professional engineer who performed
complicated calculations to the little child who
passed out food and drink.

CONTENTS

[Wendy Bell, PositivelyWendyBell.com
Photo by Alexis Fatalsky.]

Wendy Bell is a 21-time Emmy Award winner, with four Edward R. Murrow Awards and a drawer full of other accolades for the stories she has told and the newscasts she anchored during her 24 years on local and national television. She is the heart and brains behind *Positively Wendy Bell*, an online community and subscription magazine that reaches millions of people with a mission of creating an environment that changes the narrative of news by reporting meaningful and uplifting stories people want to share with their children and talk about at work.

FOREWORD

God only knows what I had done to wrench my neck. I'd walked around for days looking like a question mark, but that sweaty summertime Thursday was officially it. I needed a chiropractor. Stat. I'm not a big doctor person, believing instead that time can heal most wounds, but with small children at home and a full time job as a TV news anchor and reporter, time wasn't on my side. I needed help.

The doctor's fingers dug into a searing knot deep in my back, and I was considering screaming when my phone rang, saving me from the embarrassment. There was an emergency. And the station needed me. NOW.

The hours and days that followed that call would capture not just America's attention, but the world's. I'd never covered a story with so many lives on the line. Nine men were trapped 240 feet below the surface of the earth in a coal mine about an hour outside of Pittsburgh. And that wasn't the worst of it. The mine was flooding. As an underground reservoir of cold water poured into the precious air pockets those men needed to survive, media from around the world gathered in the parking lot of a defunct grocery store, establishing satellite connections and popping up brightly colored tents with network logos to spare the news crews from the blistering July sun. America held its breath.

I'd never heard of the Quecreek Mine before. I knew southwestern Pennsylvania was rich with natural resources and that coal mining was good, steady work in these parts. Dangerous as hell, too. I pulled into the grocery store parking lot and marveled at the media circus setting up shop. I recognized some network faces and an assortment of reporters from the local stations, but there were also Asian reporters broadcasting for some media outlets overseas, speaking so quickly and breathlessly that I thought for sure I had missed something big. I hurriedly grabbed my jug of ice water, a pen, and my notepad and raced to find my colleagues. By this time, they would already been broadcasting nonstop for a full 36 hours.

[The former Giant Eagle grocery store parking lot served as the media staging area during the rescue. Photo courtesy of Commonwealth Media Service.]

I had never experienced anything like that scene before. We reporters were all there covering the same news, trying at first to scoop each other with morsels of information from the weary woman heading the Department of Environmental Protection. But something remarkable happened inside that sparsely lit shell of an old grocery store. We started sharing information and joining forces to tell a story each of us feared would end in heartache. How often do trapped coal miners survive more than 70 hours underground? With no food, no way to communicate with the rescuers above them, and with their oxygen supplies dwindling? Women in town lit candles. American flaps unfurled with a whip in the muggy evening heat.

And the clock ticked on.

I can tell you with every honest fiber of my soul that what happened next—as the world held its collective breath—confirmed everything I loved about being a journalist. The Quecreek Mine Rescue would become the stuff of movies. Of Hollywood. Of exhausted rescuers working without rest. Of nine men prepared to die. Joined at their hips by rope so they would die together, so the rising water wouldn't wash their bodies away. Of frantic wives, and mothers, and children, pacing helplessly. Of a young dairy farmer whose land would soon become forever hallowed.

Turn the page now and lose yourself in the remarkable recounting of history, told by that dairy farmer whose life, too, was forever changed at Quecreek. Bill Arnold is more than a proud neighbor, an honorable American, and a tireless worker. He is a gifted storyteller who was there for every grueling minute of this incredible, unfolding story that you are about to read.

I remember being on live television for 24 hours that hot summer day. And I'll never forget the roller coaster of emotions. Fear. Agony. Joy. Pride. The Miracle at Quecreek Mine changed my life forever.

You know, it's funny. I don't remember feeling that searing knot in my neck for one single minute of that remarkable July day. It's almost as if something magical happened. Something so much bigger than me. Bigger than you. Bigger than *us*. We had all witnessed a miracle.

As I drove that lonely country road back to my family in Pittsburgh, completely exhausted, it all became so perfectly clear. I counted scores of American flags proudly basking in the sun outside farmhouses and businesses and tiny little cottages. Their glorious stars representing faith. The red and white stripes—the glue holding us together.

We Are America. Land of the Free. And for a brief moment in the lush countryside and rolling hills of western Pennsylvania, we were united by a single, common goal: To bring nine men blackened by coal ash and soaked to their cores back up to dry land and into the loving arms of their families.

Wendy Bell

[Dormel Farms, Somerset, Pennsylvania 2017. Photo by Bill Arnold.].

PREFACE

When my parents married in 1954, I'm sure the words "leaving a legacy" never crossed their minds, but that's exactly what they did. First, with the farm that bears their names. When Dad started dairy farming on our 18th century farm, the Holstein Association told him he needed a farm prefix to register cattle. Dad said he had to put his lady first. He took the first three letters of Mom's name (Dorcas) and the first three letters of his name (Melvin) and came up with *Dormel Farms*. When I returned to dairy farming in 1986, I continued the legacy by using the same name.

I didn't know that would be just the beginning of the legacy of *Dormel Farms*. Sixteen years after I took over the farm an incredible story happened *under* one of our pastures; 240 feet below the surface, to be exact. It was a story of not one miracle, but many—often one right after another. The developing story of the Quecreek Mine rescue gripped the hearts of people around the world as they watched events begin to unfold that evening of July 23, 2002. After the horrors of 9/11 touched our doorstep here in Somerset County, Pennsylvania, only ten months earlier with the crash of United Airlines Flight 93, the rescue of the Quecreek miners came as a breath of fresh air for all of us.

I wanted this miraculous story to be preserved, but also wanted to give readers some insight into what it is to be a normal, common dairy farmer who, in the course of four days, was tried and tested in ways that drilled down into his own depths of faith and experience, and then was thrown into the spotlight of the nation and the world.

My story in some ways is not that different from the many other ordinary people who rose up to accomplish the extraordinary; by writing this book, I do not want the reader to think I believe myself to be the most important person in the rescue operation. Far from it. This is just my story told from my perspective. I was involved in something so miraculous that I wanted to be sure it would not be lost to posterity. Future generations need to be able to look at the events that took place here and see Who was in charge. There were hundreds of human hands involved in the rescue, but every one of those volunteers will acknowledge that without divine intervention, the rescue of all nine miners never would have happened.

It was truly a modern-day miracle in an age when the word *miracle* has lost its impact.

People say, "It was a miracle our team won the football game," or "It was a miracle this person was elected to office," or "It was a miracle this or that happened."

But then you talk to eighteen miners, and they tell you, "*This* was a *miracle*," and you know they mean it.

Talk to any of the rescuers involved and find out all the details of what went on, and you will realize the power to what took place. There can be no doubt that this was the work of the Hand of God. It wasn't what we did. It was what He did through us.

That's an amazing story.

And it's a story I want to tell.

ACKNOWLEDGMENTS

I want to express my deepest gratitude to all who participated in the rescue and everyone who has supported the memorial since the rescue. My sincerest thanks to everyone who volunteers at the Visitor's Center and to all the guests who keep this story alive by continuing to visit the rescue site.

Most of all, I want to thank God, without whom the story here at Quecreek most certainly would have ended tragically.

On a personal note:

Joyann, your work (and patience with me) on this book has been remarkable.

Leslie, our paths have now been joined, and I couldn't be happier.

Jim, Carol, and Joe, your tireless support of me and this vision has been my inspiration; Carol, "above and beyond" doesn't even begin to cover it.

Paul, Anthony, Kayla, Shannon, Dave, Mike, David, Paul, Vicky, Jennifer, Buster, Willi, Maddy, Henry, Claire, Cricket, and all the other volunteers that continue to make the rescue site run on a day-to-day basis, you have my undying gratitude.

To Anna, Sheena, and the team of volunteers that have worked tirelessly on the preparations for the 15th anniversary celebration, this event would not have taken place without you.

To the hundreds of folks that donated their time in the construction of the Educational Visitors Center.

To Wendy Bell, who has shared similar highs and detours in her life, our friendship has been such a blessing to me. You are an amazing person and push me to want to be a better person, too. Your positive inspiration has affected so many, and your contribution to this work is something that I will forever treasure. Thank you.

To Mom and Dad, my teachers, my support, and my constant guidance, I love you both more than words can say.

To my kids, I will forever love you.

Bill Arnold

PROLOGUE

At 3 p.m. on July 23, 2002, 18 miners loaded onto mantrips[1] and rode a mile and a half into the depths of the Quecreek Mine to begin working their shift. Group One continued straight down into the mains. Group Two turned off into "One Left."

Group Two included Blaine Mayhugh, Mark "Moe" Popernack, Thomas "Tucker" Foy, John Unger, John "Flathead" Phillippi, Ronald "Hound Dog" Hileman, Dennis "Harpo" Hall, Robert "Boogie" Pugh, and crew chief, Randy Fogle.

The Quecreek Mine is a small coal mine located about five miles from Somerset, Pennsylvania. Somerset County was thrust into the national spotlight on September 11, 2001, with the crash of United Flight 93 near the town of Shanksville, only nine miles as the crow flies from the Quecreek Mine. Ten months after 9/11, the county had pretty much returned to normal. No one suspected the rural community would once again be shaken to its core by near-tragedy.

At 8:45 p.m., Mark Popernack was running the remote-controlled continuous miner[2] in the Number Six entry from a short distance back.

---

1 A mantrip is a long, low-profile vehicle designed to take workers and supplies quickly in and out of mines. In most cases, riders sit reclined for the trip because the roof of the mine is not high enough for an upright position. The vehicles are either on rail or wheels.

2 The continuous miner is a large machine with a wide (over 11 feet) roller equipped with teeth capable of grinding coal and other soft ore out of seams in the earth. Below the roller, a wide gathering arm funnels the loosened coal onto a conveyor belt, which carries it to another belt device that drops the coal into a waiting shuttle to be carried to the surface. Operated by remote control, it can be pushed into a seam too dangerous for an operator to go, allowing the operator to stay a safe distance back.

It had been an uneventful shift. There was no bulging of the coal seam, no creaking or groaning to warn him of the danger that loomed only three feet farther in.

The crew was ready to move out of this entry. The plan was to stay back 300 feet from the old Saxman Mine, even though state law only mandated a safety buffer of 100 feet between active and abandoned mines. They were now within 300 feet of the old mine, or so the maps told them. They had no idea the map they were working from was wrong.

For four decades the abandoned Saxman Mine had been filling up with water—millions of gallons of water—and now the weight of that water was pressing on that three-foot seam of coal separating it from the Quecreek Mine. When the seam burst and the lights went out on Mark Popernack's mining machine, he turned his head away, thinking someone had tripped the power in the mine. He glanced back toward the seam and in his cap light, saw the 50-ton continuous miner traveling towards him in a four-foot high, 20-foot wide wall of water.

He had one second to decide which way to jump and chose the Number Seven entry. He was safe. He was also separated from the other eight men on his crew by a raging river.

On the other side of that wall of water, Dennis Hall reacted quickly to the emergency. He knew the other group of nine miners working in the mains were at a lower elevation than his crew. There was a 400-foot-long dip at the intersection of the mains and One Left. If the water reached that dip before the miners did, they wouldn't have a chance.

Hall grabbed a nearby mine phone and shouted an urgent warning to the men in the other crew.

"Major water in the mine! Get out! Get out now!"

He repeated the words over and over, never sure anyone had heard his urgent warning. The water soon shorted out the electricity, and the line went dead. The miners in the mains did hear Hall's warning, and although they couldn't hear the water yet, they had enough respect for Hall and the tone of his voice to immediately begin evacuating.

It took the crew in the mains 45 minutes to fight their way out of the mine, often in fear for their lives. Without Hall's warning none of them would have survived. Once outside, they expected to see Hall and his crew waiting for them. These men knew firsthand the conditions in the mine, and their hearts sank to think that the men who had saved their lives were now trapped 240 feet below the earth's surface.

These first miners to escape the flood were told to go home; instead, all nine stayed, and for the next four days, participated in the rescue.

Hall's urgent phone call did more than just save the lives of the first nine. In those first few critical seconds, when the phone rang in the mains, it rang simultaneously in the office above ground. The startled person answering the phone heard Hall's voice and in that moment, set in motion the rescue of "The Quecreek Nine."

WEDNESDAY 2002-07-23 • 8:45 P.M.
1 MINUTE
TRAPPED UNDERGROUND

CHAPTER ONE

INTO THE DARKNESS

Sometime before midnight on Wednesday, July 23, I ran out to the equipment shed armed with my Colt 45 and a flashlight. My dog's urgent barking had awakened me from a sound sleep, and the first thing I thought was, "Someone's trying to break into the shed."

Instead of a burglar, I found Sean Isgan and Bob Long, surveyors with CME Engineering.

"Sean, what's going on?" I said.

I'll never forget what he said to me.

"Billy, there's been an accident in the mine, and there's nine men missing. We think they're trapped under your farm."

I didn't have to think twice. "What can we do to help?"

People comment that what we did in turning our farm over to the rescuers was a great sacrifice, but I like to think anyone would have responded in the same way. Especially here in Somerset County, where everyone is quick to pitch in to help those in need.

Joe Sbaffoni, from the The Department of Environmental Protection (DEP) Deep Mine Safety Bureau, started the surveying process. When he got the call about the trapped miners, he realized that if the nine miners were still alive, the first thing they would need was fresh air. He told mine operator Dave Rebuck to get the survey started in order to pinpoint a spot to drill a six-inch shaft.

Isgan and Long used a satellite Global Positioning System (GPS) to survey from the mine entrance. At the same time, Dave Zwick of Musser Engineering, used conventional surveying. The coordinates are based on underground surveying that is done on a regular basis in the mine. Miners are trained in any emergency to go to the beltway, and the last survey point on the beltway was the Number Four entry. The surveyors had to figure out where those underground coordinates were on the surface.

The first thing Zwick had to do was locate the steel marker—a "witness stake"—he had driven into the ground the previous year. Without that marker, he could not achieve an accurate survey. As Zwick walked through a field of chest-high grass at midnight looking for this marker, he felt like he was hunting a needle in a haystack. Until he tripped over something in the grass. He aimed his flashlight on the object—it was the marker he was searching for.

He began his survey using the longest straight line he could find in order to survey quickly. That straight line just happened to be state Route 985, and he surveyed down the road and onto the farm where Sean Isgan and Bob Long were waiting with their GPS survey results.

When the two survey teams planted their markers, they were less than six inches apart.

Years later, a visitor to our farm heard this story and interrupted, questioning this point. He was Colonel David Zelenock of Shriever Air Force Base in Colorado Springs, Colorado, and was in the area visiting his parents. He has since retired, but at the time of the rescue, he was head of the GPS surveying department in Colorado Springs, Colorado, and was involved with the satellite survey at that end.

He said that in his experience two different surveys—conventional and GPS—coming from two different directions can expect an accuracy of 31 feet on the first try. He continued, "If what you're telling me is true, then God had his arms wrapped around those men."

God did indeed have his arms wrapped around those men, and in this little pasture on our farm, once home to a herd of cows, the decision was made to drill in between the two markers. The exploratory hole had three purposes. First, to see if they could even find the mine from the surface, and second to see what condition the mine was in. Was it completely flooded at that point or dry? These were their two primary concerns. And finally, if the mine was dry, were there still men down there alive?

Before they could begin drilling, however, I had a concern. When I was a kid, a small independent company put a gas line in that general area. It was so old the gas company would not show it on their map, but I knew it was there. I also knew it would take time to find it and mark off the site, and time was not something we had a lot of.

I called Dad and explained what was going on, but after so many years, he wasn't sure he could remember just where the line was either. There seemed to be only one option.

"Well, I'm going to get the backhoe out and see if I can find it with the hoe," I said.

There was silence on the other end of the phone, then Dad said, "You're going to dig down there in the middle of the night with a backhoe with no running lights and intentionally try to hit a gas line?"

"Dad, there's nine guys' lives depending on it. I'm going to risk it."

He never skipped a beat. "Let me get my pants on. I'll be over to help."

Here's another example of God's preparation for this rescue. The hydraulics on the backhoe hadn't been working for quite a while. You never really have time on a farm to work on a piece of equipment until you need it. But three weeks prior to the rescue, Dad had decided to work on the backhoe. He fixed it, and now it was the first piece of equipment we needed.

As Mark Popernack waited alone in the Number Seven entry,[3] the other eight men worked their way back to the beltway.[4] As the water rose in the 42-inch-high passage, they tried to do what the first nine men had done to escape. In between each crosscut of the mine were built "stoppings," or air returns. Doors led to these returns, and they looked like a possible avenue of safety. They didn't realize the water had already completely flooded the rest of the mine, and when they broke into the return, they went from having a four-inch air space at the top of passage to being completely underwater. They had to swim back to the next crosscut 20 feet away. The only air they could find was a slim mouth space at the roof.

They knew they'd have to go back the way they came, but now they were traveling uphill and against the current. The skin was torn off their hands from pulling themselves along on the conveyor belt while the fury of the water tried to drag them backwards. The higher elevation gave them some relief, however. It bought them some time.

Popernack had waited several hours for the water to slow down, but it didn't. He figured he was the only one left in the mine, and if he were to have any chance of survival, he had to do something. He taped J-hooks to his hands with the intention of swinging on the roof bolts and making his way across the raging river.

---

3 Mines are systematically mapped into grids of pathways branching out from the main and labeled.
4 The closest corridor leading above ground, this conveyor belt path would first descend deeper into the mine.

He made it to the second bolt and knew the next one would be his last because he couldn't hold on anymore. He turned his cap light off and closed his eyes to say a prayer for his family. When he opened his eyes, one of the blocks in the wall on the other side was pushed out. Through the hole, he saw John Phillippi motioning him to get back. Mark said that was his first miracle of the night. In another few seconds, the water would have carried him a thousand feet down the mine.

When the eight miners could not find an escape route, they decided that the least they could do was get Popernack back on their side of the water. If they were going to die, they would die together.

The miners tore down the remainder of the wall between them and the water and drove one of the scoops out into the current as far as it was safe. Then Popernack made the jump of his life. Randy Fogle said that when he heard Mark's hardhat hit the back of the bucket, he knew he had him and backed the scoop up into the crosscut.

After hours of being cold and wet, the men were in danger of hypothermia. They went up to Number Four entry and huddled beside the only heat that could be found in the mine—a roof bolting machine that was still warm from use.

Aboveground, there was a lot of work to be done before we could begin drilling, not least of which was finding that old gas line.

While we were waiting for my dad to arrive, I told Sean, "This gas line had so many leaks in the old steel line over the years that they dug it up every couple thousand feet and put a plastic liner in it. So if I'm real careful, I should be able to hit the gas line and not break it."

I saw a light bulb go off in Sean's head.

"They put the plastic liner inside the old steel line?" he asked.

"Yeah."

"Did they leave the steel line in there?"

"Yeah."

He said, "Good. While you're getting the backhoe, I'll run back to the shop and get my metal detector."

When he returned, I began excavating. The only lights I had to work by were the flashlights Sean and Dad held. Each time the backhoe swung out, Sean jumped down in the hole with his metal detector. When I had dug to a depth of five feet and Sean still couldn't detect a sign of metal, I knew we were safe.

"Go ahead and drill," I told him.

"Are you sure?"

"I'm sure. Go ahead and drill."

CHAPTER TWO

BREATH OF LIFE

THURSDAY 2002-07-24 • 2:50 A.M.
6 HOURS 5 MINUTES
TRAPPED UNDERGROUND

B artels Drilling was chosen to drill the six-inch hole, and by 2:50 a.m., he had his rig set up and was starting to drill.

"The God Who Knows All" had made preparations for the rescue many months in advance. In late June, we were in a drought, and Dad said that was the best time to drill a well. It took the drillers six hours to drill a 135-foot well. In the spring, Dad had decided to build the big green building that ended up being used to house rescue workers. By early July, we had running water, and the toilets were finished on Monday. The mine accident happened the following Wednesday.

The preparation of the building could be considered trivial, but the drilling of that vital air shaft certainly was not. Remember, in late June it took six hours to drill a 135-foot shaft for the well. When they set up to drill the air shaft, they used the same diameter drill and drilled 240 feet in an hour and forty-five minutes.

More importantly, the drillers bored 240 feet down and hit a 20-foot target dead center.

To put that in perspective, in October after the rescue, mine officials wanted to try to recover the mine. The company okayed a plan to drill down from the surface, and we let them partially drain our pond and build a road out into it because the accident happened directly under the pond.

The plan was to drill down to where the accident happened between the new mine and the old and pour a solid 10-foot block of concrete in there to seal the two mines off so it couldn't flood or seep poor air or gas.

I said, "Hey, we're good at doing this. We've done this before."

The same engineering company that used the GPS for the six-inch shaft came up and located the spot for the breach between the two mines. The same drill rig and the same drill crew came back to do the work. The mining company told them not to push. All they wanted was a nice straight hole they could pour concrete down. The only difference between this shaft and the six-inch air shaft was that this time they were drilling in the daytime.

Mark that—they used the same engineers with the same GPS and the same drill crew with the same drilling rig. They had the advantage of drilling in the daytime and the luxury of the entire day to drill it. All they needed was a hole in between the old mine and the new mine.

They missed by 45 feet.

The men were stymied, but to me it was quite clear.

"You don't have to figure too hard," I said. "Nine guys' lives aren't depending on this hole."

It was clear the air shaft was one of many miracles that saved the miners' lives during those 78 hours. After the exuberance of breaking through with the six-inch shaft, we soon realized the air in the mine was at a critical level. The first thing Joe Sbaffoni of the Deep Mine Safety

Bureau did was stick his test meter underneath the apron of the drill rig to test the air quality. A massive amount of air was blowing back up out of the mine. It was like puncturing a balloon and having the air whistle out.

At the time, there were still only about a half dozen of us on the scene, and I went up to Joe and yelled over the noise of the drill rig and air compressor.

"How is it?"

"Not good. It's eleven percent."

"Eleven percent what?" I asked.

"Eleven percent oxygen."

"Is that good or bad?"

"It's not very good," he replied.

If I had been thinking clearly, from my experience as an EMT, I would have realized that the air we breathe is around 21 percent oxygen. So the air in the mine was less than half of the normal air. The air we exhale is around 16 percent oxygen, and the miners were breathing 11 percent. The miners were certainly in a critical situation.

"If they're alive, they'll be very sleepy," Joe continued. "The important thing is there's no methane or black damp in the air coming out. That would kill them."

Our small group of rescuers backed away from the drill rig to decide what we were going to do next. Lou Bartel had his back towards the drilling rig. All at once, he spun around like he had been stung by a bee.

"Somebody hit my drill bit. Those men are alive!" he said.

There was some discussion. Others in the group felt the situation was so grave it was unlikely the miners were alive.

Lou was persistent.

"I'm telling you, someone hit my drill bit. Those men down there are alive."

Then he looked at me and said, "Billy, you heard that, didn't you?"

"Lou, I did hear something," I told him. "But I'm not a driller or a miner. I don't know what I heard."

Someone suggested it might have been a rock hitting the drill pipe.

Lou could not be convinced. "I've been running drill rigs for years," he insisted. "That wasn't a rock hitting the drill pipe."

It was decided that we would have Lou pull the drill bit back up and let some more of the air come up around so we could retest it.

When Joe retested the air, it was already up to about 13 percent oxygen. That was a good sign, and he asked Lou to hit his pipe to see if we got an answer. Someone grabbed a hammer and started to bang on the pipe continuously, but Joe stopped him.

"No. Hit three times, then listen."

He hit three times, and we listened for 20 to 30 seconds and didn't hear anything. He hit three more times, and we waited again with the same result.

I was standing there thinking, "Come on, guys. Come on. Answer."

Finally Lou said, "You know, I pulled my bit back up. There's only a 4-foot coal seam here. Maybe my bit's up so that they can't get to it. Let me drop it back down in the hole."

It was agreed.

"But go slow."

Lou dropped his bit back down about a foot. He hit the pipe three times, and we listened but didn't hear anything. He dropped back down another foot and hit three times. We listened and still didn't hear anything.

The third time, he dropped his bit down and hit his pipe three times. His last hammer strike was still echoing in the valley when we got three immediate hits back. It rang like someone hitting a bell. I can remember just pumping my fist and yelling, "Yes!"

To everyone, it was like an electrical shock; the hair even stood up on the back of my neck. The response was so clear and so immediate; it was undeniable there were men down there. From that point on, I was convinced there were nine guys to be rescued, and we were going to get all nine out.

We found out later that the 6-inch drill had broken through just in time. The miners were ready to suffocate. There was no oxygen left in the mine, and they were breathing very hard. Each of the nine has a different story. One guy said they could count the number of breaths they had left on both hands. Mark Popernack said he felt like a dog—his tongue was hanging out, and he was panting. They said they would breathe in as hard as they could, but before they could get their lungs full, they had to blow it back out and try again because it wasn't doing any good. When the drill broke through, it brought fresh air with it and saved their lives.

Once again, if anything had been out of place—if the surveyors had needed to start their process over, if the drilling had not gone smoothly, if the equipment had not been readily available—those miners would have died.

But God had it all worked out.

It turned out the compressor on Lou's drill rig was just the right type of compressor. Some compressors contaminate air. This compressor took good air from outside and pumped it down the drill steel into the mine.

Once rescuers realized the need the miners had for air, the next step was to figure out how to stop the air from blowing back up around the drill pipe. Joe Sbaffoni went to the Sipesville Fire Department and got long narrow airbags like those they use to lift cars off trapped people. They pushed those air bags down around the drill steel and inflated them. It sealed off most of the escaping air.

I was beside the shaft with some of the volunteer firemen when we inflated those air bags, and there was about a 10-foot-diameter circle of earth around the drill pipe that began to heave up from the amount of pressure we were clamping down into the mine. We all took a few steps back because we weren't sure it was going to hold. But it did.

Around lunchtime on Thursday, engineers figured that the water in the mine covered the 6-inch drill pipe and in the process sealed the bottom of the shaft. At that point, the amount of air escaping was further reduced. The air we were sending down was bubbling up through the water towards the highest point in the mine, creating an air pocket exactly where the miners were. And the water continued to rise.

CHAPTER THREE

FUELING UP

After hearing the miners pound on the pipe, I felt energized. I ran down to the house to change from the sweats I had thrown on at midnight into work clothes. I was trying to change clothes as fast as I could, and I remember hopping around on one foot while I was trying to take my sweat pants off and put jeans on. It was soon going to be daylight, and I thought, "We have all day now. We can get them out. I'll put everything else off. I'll spend all day, and we'll get those guys out."

That feeling never really left me. It took a little longer than one day, but the feeling never left, and it's something I'll never forget.

The mining engineers had a theory that the air being pumped into the mine at 300 psi would create an air pocket. It wouldn't push the water back, but the pressure would provide continuous air for the miners to breathe and possibly create an air pocket that the water couldn't penetrate. It was all theory—it had never been done before. But it was all we had.

Sbaffoni asked Lou Bartels how long he could keep his compressor running.

Lou told him, "As long as you can keep me in diesel."

From that moment, I decided that making sure he didn't run out of fuel would be my top priority. I asked Lou's son Jeremy, who had worked for me on the farm when he was in high school, if there was fuel in the tank on the back of his dad's pickup. He said there wasn't.

"How much fuel's in your dad's rig?"

"Probably less than half full."

I said, "Okay, come with me."

I took him up over the hill to my fuel tank. At this point, it seemed as if the few of us there were the only rescuers. Whatever needed to be done would be up to us to do. So I unlocked my fuel tank and told Jeremy to fill the tank on the back of his dad's truck and ferry the fuel down to his rig.

"Keep ferrying fuel in your pickup and make sure everything stays filled up with fuel. I'll have Agway keep my tank full, and we'll square up later," I told him.

When Dave, the driver for Agway Fuel, arrived, I had him fill my tank. Then I suggested that he fill my backhoe and skid loader right out of the truck. He did that and asked if I wanted him to come back with more diesel.

I said, "Yes. Keep coming until I tell you not. Keep my tank full."

When Dave returned, he asked if there was any way he could get down into the field and fill things up out of the truck. I showed him where he could drive around to get into the field, and he backed in and started filling the drill rig. I told him that was his first priority.

"Just keep the slips, Dave," I said. "Bill it to me and give the slips to me all at one time."

He shook his head. "Bill, I don't think there are any slips."

Dave came back every three hours and followed the checklist I had given him. First, he filled the drill rig. Then the compressors on the drill rig. Then my skid loader and backhoe. By his second trip, we had an excavator here, and someone brought a dozer. Air compressors started to show up, and someone dropped off a bulk fuel tank.

As the rescue progressed, more and more equipment arrived, and it became harder for Dave to keep up, especially after Yost arrived with his big, super drill rig. I let Dave know there was a new piece of equipment on site.

He said, "I'm out. I filled Yost, and I'm empty."

At one point, a second fuel company was called, and I arranged with the drivers to stagger their visits. Every hour and a half, there was a fuel truck on the site filling equipment, and that's the way they ran for the remainder of the rescue.

Somebody had to take charge of refueling and make sure it was done, because if we ran out of fuel, no one was going anywhere. When there was nothing else going on, I would walk through, check fuel levels, and check if any other equipment was coming in that would need gasoline instead of diesel, etc. That was almost a full-time job.

Yost's rig alone took an enormous amount of fuel. During the time when the bit was broken and the drill rig was just idling, I still put about a thousand gallons of fuel in their rig just to keep them from running out. When they were drilling and using a lot of fuel, we were probably dumping 5,000 to 7,000 gallons in the rig every three hours.

One of the essential people involved in the rescue was Larry Neff, a consultant with Bethlehem Energy Mines. He looked like a cross between actor Ed Harris and President John F. Kennedy. With stone gray hair and piercing blue eyes, he had stunning good looks. He was trim and very squared away, even in work shirt and blue jeans. I suspect his wife pressed his blue jeans for him to go out and work on the farm.

It was just about daylight Thursday morning when he showed up. We were working fast and furious once that 6-inch drill bit went through and we heard the men hitting on it.

Jim Svonavec had already excavated a huge hole when Neff showed up and started directing the placement of the casing pipe and the pouring of concrete and stone in the hole. During a break, when one concrete truck was pulling out and another one started to pull in, I ran the skid loader up, shut it off, and motioned for Larry to come over.

I stuck out my hand and said, "I'm Bill Arnold. I own the farm here."

He said, "I'm Larry Neff."

"I'm trying to keep things straight here. Are you state, DEP, or MSHA?"

He smiled and said, "I'm just a farmer like you."

He paused a moment, and I guess by the way I kept looking at him he knew I wanted more of an explanation, so he added, "I'm a consultant with Beth Energy Mine."

After the pipe was set, there was a break in the action, and I had another opportunity to talk to Larry.

"So you're a farmer, huh?" I said.

And we started to talk about his farm down in Summerhill and discovered we had a lot of friends in common.

"How did you find out about this?" I asked.

"I was at home, and I heard about the accident on the news. I was pacing back and forth and couldn't go to sleep. I was wondering what I could do to help."

Some time later the phone rang, and it was Duane Yost. Larry had worked with Duane and his dad many times over the years.

Duane said, "Larry, you're the only guy who doesn't work for me that I trust to set our pipe. Can you go up and set our pipe so we're not screwing around for eight hours once we get there?"

"No one's asked me to leave yet," Neff concluded with a smile. "So I just thought maybe I'd stick around to see if I could help."

During the course of the rescue, as I had opportunity to observe people, I noticed they all gave Neff a great deal of respect. You just knew Neff was in charge. There was something in the way he carried himself, but it wasn't arrogance or hardheadedness. It was like an aura.

I even asked a few people. I went to one guy with DEP and said, "I'm just asking so when this all hits the fan, I know. Who's in charge here, anyway?"

His answer was almost identical to everyone else's answer. "See that little guy down there in the white hat. That's Neff. He's the man."

Larry didn't come on the property and announce he was in charge. No one took a vote. It was just a matter of fact. That was the respect his management skills engendered in everyone.

And what an awesome job he did. He always knew exactly what was going on. He was thinking at least 24 hours ahead of where he was right now. He had four different possible scenarios worked out in his head, and he knew how he would resolve each scenario if it did happen.

Yet there were no airs with Larry Neff. His down-to-earth manner was exemplified by the watch he kept in his pocket. It wasn't a pocket watch. It was a wristwatch. He carried it in his pocket because half of the band was missing. That didn't mean it wasn't a good watch. It kept good time, so he carried it in his pocket. Who needs a new watch or a new wristband when this one works perfectly fine? You'd see him stop and reach in that pocket, check the time, then put it back in his pocket.

That was the essence of Larry Neff.

CHAPTER FOUR

SETTING UP

The Yost Drilling Company, from Greene County, Pennsylvania, had the huge RD-50 super drill that was needed to drill the rescue shaft. Their rig was at a site in West Virginia, but upon receiving the call, it was dismantled and trucked across two states. We had a lot of work to do, however, before the rig arrived.

When we heard the miners hit the drill steel, we knew their approximate location. We didn't want to stray very far from that spot. We just backed up 20 feet from the 6-inch shaft and prepared to set the casing.

As a farmer and a contractor in business, I had built a milking parlor about three years before the accident happened, so I had contracts with various supply companies. That was helpful in getting the rescue initiated because they had me in their computers. They could bring my account up and get directions to the farm.

This is when I began to see the community—not only of Somerset, but of the state and country—pull together to do whatever it took to rescue those men.

When Larry Neff said they were going to set up for a rescue shaft and would need some pipe, I thought, "This is good. I got pipe."

He told me they would need pipe 20 feet long.

I said, "I got it covered. What do you need? One inch? Two inch? Two and a half? I got 3-inch pipe. What do you need?"

He said, "We'll need pipe 36 inches in diameter."

That was a little bigger than what I had here, but I could get it.

"How thick does it have to be?"

"At least three-eighths."

I figured I would go to Marmon Steel, the biggest supplier out of Pittsburgh. It was two or three in the morning when I placed the call, and the phone rang and rang. I kept thinking, "There has to be someone there."

The phone rang maybe twenty times until finally, someone answered.

I said, "This is Bill Arnold in Somerset. This is an emergency. There's nine men's lives on the line. I need pipe, and I need it right now."

After a long pause, she replied in a heavy Spanish accent, "I'm the cleaning lady."

I thought, "She going to think I'm some kind of a kook and hang up on me."

I said, "Ma'am, please don't hang up the phone. There's an emergency in Somerset, Pennsylvania. I have an account there. We need pipe, and we need it immediately. You have to have a contact number. A manager. A night foreman. The owner. Please write this information down and contact them. We need pipe 20 feet long, 36 inches in diameter, with three-eighth-inch wall thickness or better."

She said, "Wait, I don't understand. I'm the cleaning lady."

I said, "Just write this down. Twenty feet long."

I waited.

"Okay," she said.

"Thirty-six inches in diameter."

"Okay."

"Three-eighth-inch wall thickness."

She said, "I don't understand what that means."

"Write the fraction 'three-eighths'. And then 'thickness.' Please do the best you can."

I gave her my cell phone number and went on down my list. I wasn't sure if my message was going to get through to anyone in Pittsburgh, so I also called companies in Altoona, Greensburg, and Stoystown. By the time I returned to the rescue site, my cell phone was ringing.

The guy on the other end said, "This is the owner of Marmon Steel in Pittsburgh. Your pipe is on its way."

He got the driver out of bed, and they had the truck loaded by the time the driver showed up. The pipe was on the site in less than an hour. The "cleaning lady" did a great job.

By daylight Thursday morning, in response to my call to other distributors, we had 20 pieces of pipe here. As it turned out, only one of those pipes wasn't used over the course of the rescue.

The first necessity, however, was to case the drill hole. Until you get down to bedrock, the topsoil in a hole is likely to cave in. You can get away without a casing in a 6-inch hole because it's not going to cave in too much, but when you're drilling a 30-inch hole, you've got a lot of ground there that's really unstable.

[Setting the casing for the first rescue shaft. Bill Arnold is operating the skidloader (left). Photo courtesy of Dormel Farms.]

Jim Svonavec showed up with his excavator and started digging the hole for the casing. When he reached 20 feet, we set the casing in and made sure it was plumb. We started pouring fast—setting concrete in on the side of the hole closest to the casing. Of course, the concrete wanted to run around the pipe to the other side of the hole. If we had tried to fill the entire area with concrete, it would have taken 20 truckloads. Instead, I was trying to dump stone in with my skid loader at the same rate as the concrete in order to fill up the hole. This way it only took four truckloads of concrete.

At the time, this was the fastest way to get the casing set. By the time we started drilling the second rescue shaft, we had more equipment. Nearby there was a rig that was digging starter holes with an auger bit. He came and used that 36-inch auger to bore the second hole. When he hit 20 feet, he pulled the bit out and placed a special tool on the bottom of the bit that clamped onto the top of the casing. He picked the casing up and set it down into the ground. The job was done in an hour, whereas it took us four to five hours to get Rescue One set up.

Late Thursday morning, Duane Yost, son of owner Gene Yost, pulled his huge drill rig onto our farm. The whole trip up he had worried about how far back in this farmer's field the site would be, and how would he ever get his big rig in? But here it was, right next to the main road, and he was ready to set up his big sub-frame—like a big steel H—around the casing. This creates a stable platform upon which he could back the wheels of the drill rig. All this would take several hours, but then he could set up his boom and prepare to drill.

[An American flag flew atop of the Falcon rig as it drilled the second rescue shaft.]

Another issue that had to be dealt with was the amount of material that would be coming out of the rescue shaft. Enormous amounts of ground, limestone, foam, and water would be discharged in the course of drilling a 30-inch shaft 240 feet into the earth.

Larry Neff asked me where the field drained to. I told him it went down to the end of the field, into a culvert under the road, into a stream and eventually into Quecreek.

He said, "We're going to have an awful lot of material coming out of this drill site, and we're going to be dumping it out on top of the ground."

"If that's the case, we're going to be up to our waists in water," I told him. "The pipe under the road was put in 50 or more years ago, and it's only an 8-inch culvert. If we start washing a bunch of material down there and plug that hole, we're going to be in a lake here."

He suggested straw bales to trap the heavier material out of the water, and I asked him how long I had to do it. At that point, he estimated two to three hours before they could actually begin drilling. I told him I would get something done.

I called Lynn Baer from New Enterprise Stone and Lime Company. I've known Lynn since junior high, and I told him I needed five truckloads of Number 4 stone, three truckloads of Number 3's, and probably a couple of truckloads of 2-B.

He said, "I've got a couple of trucks already loaded. I'll send them out. As soon as I can get drivers in the seats, I'll get the others loaded and get them out there."

We proceeded to build a coffer dam.[5] First, we put down the really big stones. Number 4 stone is the size of a basketball. We made a horseshoe-shaped barricade at the lower end of the field so that when the water and heavy ground-up limestone came out, it would hit the barricade and slow it down enough to let the heaviest materials drop out. The water and foam and fine ground-up material would pass through.

In the next section we put the Number 3's and after that the shale. Each time the water hit a barrier, it would slow down enough to let the material settle out and the water on through.

While they were dumping the stone, I called Bob Hay and told him I needed about 50 small square bales of straw. Bob is the manager at Lincoln Supply, and he ended up helping a lot with the rescue. He was also a friend and neighbor. Bob told me he had what I needed, but his

---

5 A coffer dam is a temporary wall or enclosure built into a body of water to divert either water or soil. Usually constructed to allow work to be done in a dry area, this dam's purpose was to slow and filter debris-filled water in order to prevent clogging in the narrow drain path.

guys were scattered all over the county helping with other aspects of the rescue. I told him I would take care of it.

I don't even remember who I asked, but I grabbed someone and told him to take my pickup and go over to Bob Hay's Shaffer barn and get me as many straw bales as he could get on the truck without losing any. He brought the straw, and that was the last barrier the water had to go through. It trapped the water one final time to allow the finest material to drop out. This prevented the drainpipe under the highway from getting blocked up.

It was a minor issue in the course of the rescue, but if we had plugged that pipe, it would have severely hindered the drilling process.

When Duane Yost pulled in with his rig, he told us that in four hours he would be ready to drill.

"If you want to communicate with these men, you need to do it before I start this drill."

After the drill was started, not only would there be the noise of the air compressing into the 6-inch shaft, there would also be the sound of the 30-inch bit striking 500 times a minute. When it started up, the pressure of the hammer on the ground could be felt for hundreds of yards away.

Jeff Stanchek was a mine rescue instructor. He had taught these men what to do in the event of a mine emergency. He knew the men could survive if they got what they needed: air and a way out. The consensus was that we needed to communicate with the miners somehow so we would know that they were still alive and how many of them there were.

At 11:30 a.m., they decided to attempt communication and silence was essential. By this time there were more than 200 people on the site, and the order went out to maintain silence. Everyone was asked to sit down on the ground because seismograph had been set up all around the area, and they didn't want anyone shuffling their feet or moving around. The seismic equipment was very sophisticated. They plugged microphones into the ground that—theoretically—would enable them to hear a man walking in a mine 1,000 feet down.

One of my favorite stories of that morning was told to me by a local firefighter. One of the U.S. Department of Labor's Mine Safety and Health Administration (MSHA) officials approached him and said, "Fireman, we're doing this test and everything needs to be perfectly still. We need you to go up the hill to this farmer's herd of cattle and make them stand still and not make any noise."

The fireman told me, "What was I supposed to do? This was a federal guy. I'm just a volunteer fireman. Was I supposed to tell him, 'You're an idiot'?"

He walked up to my field, praying, "How am I supposed to do this? God, I need a little help here."

When he reached my field, he said it was as if my cows had turned into statues. Every one of them froze and stared at him for ten minutes.

He said, "I'm a farm boy. I know that doesn't happen. All I could do was stand there and cry."

Forty-five head of cattle stayed perfectly still for ten minutes. That is a miracle.

We were to experience many more miracles from that time on.

Back at the drill site, the workers were ready to try to communicate, and a hammer was given to Tony Gibbons. He smacked the drill steel.

It turned out the miners had retreated back to the only place in the whole mine where there was no water. Every now and then, a couple of them would go back and check the air shaft, so it took a few minutes for the men to come to the drill bit and answer our summons.

According to mine rescue protocol, the signals were given in succession.

Tony gave the drill three smacks.

The answer came back: three pings.

Then five smacks.

And the answer: five pings.

Seven smacks.

By this time, the trapped miners apparently lost patience with protocol and went straight to nine pings.

And when the nine pings were heard from deep beneath the earth's surface, cheers broke out across the little valley.

Jeff Stanchek ran up the hill through the excited rescuers and screamed through his tears, "They will live! They will live, because they know how!"

We had been hearing pings from the miners consistently since 6 a.m. that morning. That was the last time we would hear from them for almost 60 hours.

THURSDAY 2002-07-24 11:30 A.M.
14 HOURS 45 MINUTES
TRAPPED UNDERGROUND

Depth = 160'
D.T.C. = 122'
40' casing
50 gpm
Sperry drilling 5-02

164

AREA

14A

14B

14

W   SP105

Depth = 150'
D.T.C. = 90'

Escape Well

X 2054.1

100

SR35

Depth = 14
D.T.C. = 19

100A

23H

2069.2

WE

Rescue #1

18

X 2098.0

Depth = 230'
D.T.C. = 90'

23F
23G

SP11
W

X 2073.5

23E

23A

SP180

23B

W

23C   23D

NO MINING

SP103

WE

2076.8

SP103

Depth = 135'
D.T.C. = 115'

1820

Depth = 165'

CHAPTER FIVE

DRILLING INTERLUDE

E ven as we prepared the rescue site and Yost's drill rig roared into life, additional crews had been working for hours at multiple sites in the area, boring drill holes to pump water out of the mine. It has been estimated that 220,000 gallons of water a minute were pouring out of the old Saxman Mine—that's the equivalent of eleven backyard swimming pools—and the Quecreek Mine entrance was under 18 feet of water.

If the rescuers were going to lower the water level in the mine, they would need enormous pumps, and some of them were provided by God Himself.

Two pumps, each capable of pumping at a rate of 3,000 gallons of water a minute, had been on their way to the state of Indiana. The driver stopped in Somerset overnight, and when he got up Thursday morning, he intended to get back on the turnpike to finish the delivery.

He heard on the CB there had been a mine accident at Quecreek involving a lot of water, and the men were probably going to drown. This driver took it upon himself to find out how to get to Quecreek. When he pulled in at the farm, he stopped right in the middle of the road.

I went out to meet him, jumped up on the side of the truck, and said, "Buddy, what do you got?"

He said, "Look, I'm probably going to get fired, because these aren't your pumps, but I thought maybe you could use them. Where do you want them?"

I said, "I don't know. This isn't the mine. Turn around at the barn and take them straight across the road, and you'll run into the mine. They'll know what to do with them."

They put both of those pumps on line, and they turned out to be one of the deciding factors in the fight to lower the water level.

The amazing thing is, those pumps were on the road long before the accident in the mine happened.

There was also a 7,000-gallon-a-minute pump headed across country. The governor of New Jersey gave them orders to go to Somerset. That pump was also ordered several days prior to the accident. Once again, God had prepared for the miracle.

When that truck crossed the border between New Jersey and Pennsylvania, it was met by the Pennsylvania State Police.

The officer pulled him over and asked, "What will this truck do?"

The driver thought for a moment, silently wondering if this was some sort of speed trap. Finally, he said, "Oh, it'll probably do 90."

The state trooper said, "Let's do that. Do 90."

The truck had a state trooper escort the whole way. When they left one jurisdiction, that trooper would drop off, and another one would pick the truck up. The truck crossed the state line around midnight and pulled in at the farm around 3:00 a.m. Thursday morning.

By 9:15 a.m., several pumps were set up and working to pump water out of the mine.

At the height of the pumping, water was coming out of the mine at a rate of 36,000 gallons of water per minute. That's approximately equivalent to one Olympic-sized swimming pool (660,000 gallons) every 18 minutes. That's the amount it took to not only stop the water in the mine from rising, but to begin to drop the water levels a quarter of an inch every hour. The guys at the mine said it wasn't much, but it was going in the right direction. It only took 50 million gallons of water to fill the Quecreek Mine to the roof, but as the water was being pumped out, the mine was continually re-flooding because the water source in the old Saxman Mine was continually refilling that mine. It was like trying to empty the ocean with a bucket. After pumping 150 million gallons out of the active mine, the water level in the Saxman Mine had only dropped nine feet.

The water created another problem. Rescuers realized that if the air pocket theory worked, the trapped men would be under a lot of pressure. The air going down the 6-inch shaft and bubbling up through the water to the men only had a 70-foot space to fill. The water was compressing the air into that small space to such a degree that when the men were brought up they could potentially suffer from the bends, just like a deep-sea diver. The possibility existed that we would have to bring them up under pressure.

That's why the Navy Seals were here, along with the Navy Underwater Construction and Demolition teams. The Navy medical personnel stood ready with the decompression chambers because they said it would be very much like a submarine rescue.

With this in mind, an airlock was designed by local and Navy engineers right here on the site. The blueprints were drawn with fingertips on dusty truck hoods and on notebooks pulled out of hip pockets. Don and Buddy Walker, of nearby Lincoln Contracting, were instrumental in the construction of the 40-foot-long, 36-inch-diameter tube that would serve as an airlock.

If we would have had to use the airlock, workers would first have to install it on top of the hole after they broke through into the mine—a process that would have taken 12 to 18 hours. An air compressor would have maintained pressure in the hole while the drill bit was removed through the airlock pipe. At that point, a crane would have raised the rescue capsule and lowered it into the airlock, after which the lid would have been re-bolted in place.

[The U.S. Navy decompression chambers that were brought on-site in case they were needed. Photo courtesy of Commonwealth Media Service.]

Now they would be ready for the actual rescue. The airlock would have to be pressurized to the same level as the air being pumped into the mine. The knife valve at the bottom of the airlock would open, and the capsule would be lowered into the mine. A miner would enter the capsule through a side door, and the capsule/airlock would return to the surface. Once on the surface, the knife valve would be closed, and the pressure inside the airlock would be released. Once the pressure in the airlock was equalized with surface pressure, we could open the door on the side of the airlock and take the man out of the capsule. The airlock would then need to be re-pressurized, and the process repeated eight more times.

The estimated time for each man's rescue would have been one hour. As it turned out, the rescue shaft's stability became a concern, and it may not have survived the nine hours required to remove nine men. Keep this in mind as you read the next few chapters. Once again, God knew what we needed better than we did.

[The portable decompression chamber is shown in the back of the truck. Photo courtesy of Commonwealth Media Service.]

Putting that airlock together on site was no small feat. We used two of the 20-foot pipes we had lying here. I used the skid loader to try to push the pipes together. They weren't square, and they weren't round, and here we were trying to route egg-shaped pipes together. The welder I was working with was filling 2-inch gaps with his welder. He'd get a tack, then he'd motion me to try and squeeze the pipes together so he could weld it. I was holding it as best I could with the skid loader and shut my eyes while he welded. When the flash would quit, I'd open my eyes, and he'd motion me forward or back, and then he'd finish the welding.

This poor guy was in the same boat I was in. People were telling us to do things, and we didn't know why we were doing them. At one point, he'd had all he could take.

Larry Neff was explaining to this welder what needed done next.

"We need to make sure this is perfectly square, because we need to attach this airlock to the top of the rescue shaft and be able to slide this valve in here, and it needs to be able to seal. So it has to be square, and it has to be true."

At this point, the welder, who like the rest of us had probably been up at least 24 hours, hit the wall. He was being asked to fabricate something when he didn't even know what it was or how it was going to be used. And he'd had it.

He threw his helmet down and said, "I don't know what the hell you expect me to do. I'm down here in waist-deep grass with no lights, welding pipes that don't fit together on rough ground. Nothing matches up square, and I don't even know what I'm building."

Larry's character really shone through when faced with this frustrated welder.

He reached over, put a hand on the man's shoulder, and said, "Son, you're a good man. These guys are counting on us to get them out. I have faith in you. Just do your best."

The guy thought for a second, then stood up a little taller and looked at me.

He reached down, picked up his helmet, and said, "Let's get to work.

That was it. I looked at Larry and thought, "Wow, that was pretty incredible." And I swear, I think Larry winked at me before I turned to follow the welder.

That was the way people just showed up here and pitched in. I remember early Friday morning, I needed to move some drill steels from

Bartel's rig out of the way. I had moved them once, and now they were on the spot where we were going to need to put Falcon's drill rig for the second rescue hole.

I was looking around for the 6-foot chain I always keep on my skid loader. Apparently, someone had taken it and not put it back. I needed to chain these 20-foot pipes onto my pallet forks to move them.

While I'm looking around, a pickup truck pulled in. There were three guys in the cab and maybe four guys in the bed. I didn't know who they were or what mine they worked at. In fact, I still don't know who they were.

These men looked like they had been dipped in ink, and I remember thinking, "This is a coal miner. This is what a coal miner looks like."

The only thing you could see on them that wasn't black were the whites of their eyes, their teeth, and the blue work shirts and pants they wore. It was kind of eerie.

These guys jumped out of the pickup and looked around as though sizing up the situation.

They saw me looking for my chain, and one of them said, "Buddy, whaddya need?"

I said, "I'm looking for my chain. It's not on my skid loader. I've gotta move these drill steels."

He said, "We'll do it."

I said, "Guys, you can't lift them. They weigh a ton. I need my chain so I can move them with my machine."

The man looked back at the rest of his guys and gave a nod of his head, as though he hadn't heard a word I'd said. They walked over, grabbed a drill steel, picked it up, threw it up on their shoulders, and started to walk away with it just like it was a toothpick.

As the one who had originally talked to me walked past me, he said, "Where do you want them?"

I pointed. "Just take them down there and lay them in a stack."

As the men continued to file past, he looked back at me and said, "Get it done. Those men are our brothers."

Those miners were willing to do whatever it took. Or were they miners? The book of Hebrews talks about entertaining angels unaware. Could it be?

Two of the most common questions we get here have to do with the pond water. People want to know whether the water in the pond is the water they pumped out of the mine, or if the accident caused the pond to drain.

It might seem odd, but we didn't pump any flood water into the farm pond at all. We were actually hauling water in, using a tractor-trailer-sized tank that held 10,000 gallons of water.

Drillers drill dry until they hit water. At around 100 feet down, they hit aquifers and of course, that produces mud. To compensate for this, they pump water down, flood the hole completely and add a sort of biodegradable, industrial-strength dish washing liquid. The air from the compressor blows down through the drill steel and bubbles up through the water to make foam. That foam helps lift the ground-up rock, shale, and gravel to the top of the hole, and when it gets to the flow pipe, it blows out the exhaust. Water also helps cool the bit and provides lubrication. The water tank was parked at the top of the hill, and the firefighters hauled water down to the drill site to keep the tank full. Hoses ran down over the hill to feed water by gravity for the drillers to flood their holes.

This procedure isn't necessary for the smaller drill rigs. They just blow things right up underneath the rig and have rubber aprons around to keep it from blowing all over the place. When it starts to pile up, they shovel it away. The big drill rigs bring up such a massive amount of material that they need to blow it out the flow pipe and try to get it away from the drill shaft.

Drilling had been going on for eight hours, and we were feeling pretty good about the situation. Governor Schweiker was projecting "break-through" times.

At one point, I asked the tool pusher, Sean, "How deep?"

He said, "One hundred feet."

"How long 'til you break through?"

"Eight to ten hours."

[Governor Mark Schweiker and the Department of Environmental Protection's Joe Sbaffoni update the media. Photo courtesy of Commonwealth Media Service.]

It was early Friday morning, and I hadn't slept since Wednesday night. I thought this was a good opportunity to get some rest so I would be fresh when they broke through. I only got one boot off when I got word.

At 105 feet, the drill bit hit a seam of sandstone and sheared off.

FRIDAY 2002-07-25 1:50 A.M.
29 HOURS 5 MINUTES
TRAPPED UNDERGROUND

CHAPTER SIX

BROKEN BITS

When the bit broke, it was decided almost immediately to set up for a second hole.

Neff came to me and said, "We're going to need that equipment moved down in the bottom part of the field."

I said, "Why?"

He said, "Sometimes it takes two weeks for these guys to get a bit out of a hole. Sometimes they never do. I don't want to take that chance; we're going to start a new hole right now."

The drill bit was 30 inches in diameter, in a 36-inch casing. The rescuers tried every technique they knew to try to pull the bit out, but there was no room around it to clamp onto it. George Sonnie of Sunrise Drilling Supply even fabricated a makeshift overshot and attempted to retrieve the bit. But all attempts failed.

A location was plotted 70 feet from Rescue One.

The rig for Rescue Two was pulled in from the cornfields where it was drilling holes for pumps. It was described to me as a bigger rig than Yost's, but not as powerful. It could drill Rescue Two, but drilling to 240 feet would be at that rig's uppermost limit. It would get the job done, but just barely.

As the drilling on the second hole progressed, rescuers desperately wanted to be able to complete the first hole for the rescue. First of all, the miners knew where the 6-inch hole was, and they would be checking that area. Also, the first hole would break through at the highest elevation in the mine. The mine entrance still had 18 feet of water in it and was about 21 feet higher than the air pocket, so we knew that when the water started to go down, this higher elevation would be cleared first.

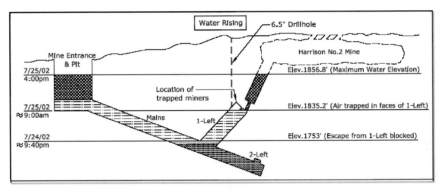

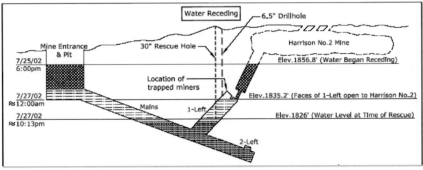

[Quecreek #1 mine simplified cross-section showing rise and fall of water levels. Map photo courtesy of Bill Arnold,.]

In spite of the setback, we weren't going to accept anything but success from the get-go. It was a long haul, but I can remember never losing faith. During the darkest hours of the rescue, when both drill bits were broken, I can remember one specific instance of taking time to drop to a knee and say a prayer. It wasn't a prayer that the miners would be okay. I wasn't asking God for them to live—to me that was a given. I was asking God to give them the strength and patience they would need until we got to them.

For me, it seemed as though God had already told us the miners were all going to make it. It was only a matter of time. If I would have known then what I know now about the complexities of the mine and the situations they were dealing with, I probably wouldn't have been as faithful. I was fortunately naive to the conditions they were in.

A couple of times when I tried to sit down and eat or rest a few moments, it occurred to me—if this is what I feel like, what are those men in the mine going through? Possibly injured, cold, wet, hungry. And then my tiredness would fade away, and I would become energized and get up and start checking on equipment and checking fuel levels on rigs and go to the guys who were in charge of different things and say, "Okay, where are we at? What are we going to need next?" My goal was to look for potential problems and try to head them off before they occurred.

There was one other concern I needed to take care of. Other types of businesses can shut down for a few days, and although they'll lose money in the process, there's no urgency to remain open. It's not that simple on a farm. The cows had to be milked no matter what other crisis was occurring.

My 15-year-old neighbor boy had been helping me out and on Thursday morning when he arrived, I said to him, "Listen, you're going to have to take over the cows. Treat them as if they were your cows. Do the milking and the feeding and take care of the animals. That's all you need to do. I'm going to depend on you. If you need me, come and find me."

He said, "There's a state cop out at the end of the road, and he yells at me that I'm not allowed back here."

"Don't worry about that," I told him. "I'll take care of the state trooper. You just tell him you're working on the farm and milking the cows. If he gives you any trouble, you let me know."

The boy reacted as though I had just promoted him to general. I spoke to the state trooper about letting the boy in, and I also discussed the need to let the milk truck in. At that time, my milkman was coming around nine p.m. I called Philip and said, "Listen, I think it's probably best that you come as late as possible. Maybe by then we'll get this thing squared away. If not, at least there won't be as many people standing around, and you won't have as much trouble getting your truck in and out."

We agreed that he would come close to midnight and would call when he was fifteen minutes away so I could let the state troopers know and get the road cleared for him.

I think he had to make three pick-ups during the rescue. He never once said to me, "Hey, my brother-in-law is one of the trapped miners."

It took me several days to realize that Philip's sister was miner John Unger's wife.

I asked him later why he didn't say anything.

He said, "I was hoping you didn't know. You didn't need any more pressure on you."

His selfless spirit was repeated by many others over the course of the four days.

Governor Mark Schweiker was wonderful during the entire rescue. From the time he arrived on the scene Thursday evening, he informed everyone this was a rescue, not a recovery. He promised to put every resource of the state at the rescuers' disposal, and he was as good as his word.

He also insisted on keeping the families at the Sipesville Fire Hall informed—even when that meant telling them the drill bit had broken.

It was a low moment for everyone involved, and the weather seemed like a reflection of our spirits. Up to this time, it had been sunny and clear. In fact, we had just had a three-month drought, but when the bit broke, the clouds came in and it became damp and dreary. Tents were set up for shelter, and you could almost feel the discouragement.

My first encounter with Governor Schweiker was less than memorable.

Another fuel truck had just pulled in, and I was in the process of filling things up. I was pulling a couple hundred feet of 2-inch fuel hose, and that's a lot of weight. Out of the corner of my eye, I saw this hustle and bustle, and I looked up and saw a clean-cut, debonair man walking around. He was smiling and giving hugs and patting people on the back and shaking hands.

I was irritated, and remember thinking, "I thought they ran the reporters out of here."

I happened to glance up to the top of the hill and saw my mom. I heard her yelling, "Bill! Bill!" She was pointing to this guy, and I looked at him and looked back at her, and she just kept pointing to him. We were far enough away that she couldn't really yell too much. So I just went back about my business.

As the man came down to the rescue site, I wasn't offensive to him, but I didn't have time to chat with him either, so I just sort of brushed my way by him. He let me pass, shook a few more hands, then went back up to the top of the hill and disappeared.

When I finally got a few minutes to go up to the top of the hill, Mom was waiting for me, dancing around like a schoolgirl.

She said, "Don't you know who that was?"

I'm thinking, "Gee, he must have been in a soap opera or something, if Mom's that excited about him."

I said, "No. Who was it?"

"That's the governor."

I said, "Well, Mom, I really didn't have time to talk to him. I was busy with the fuel."

Late that night I had the opportunity to meet the governor and make amends.

I said to him, "By the way, Governor, I wasn't very courteous to you earlier when you were here. I didn't mean any offense. I didn't realize it was you."

He was very gracious about the whole thing.

At the time, I was still thinking he was here for political reasons, rather than for the absolute right reasons. He wasn't an elected governor. Only nine months earlier, he had been lieutenant governor, and was elevated to governor when Tom Ridge was appointed as director of the newly formed Office of Homeland Security. As we learned over the course of the rescue, Governor Schweiker's motivation for spending those four days here was absolutely true and honorable.

He wasn't the only one. At one point, after Rescue One's drill bit broke, one of the Navy Seals came up to me and said, "Look, everyone on my team is certified for underwater welding. Tie us by our ankles and drop us down that hole, and we'll weld the damn thing back on."

I looked at him and said, "By your ankles?"

He said, "Yes. We're trained to work blind."

Well, I passed it up the chain of command, and everyone reacted pretty much as I had.

"You're serious?"

And the guy's standing right there: "Yes. We're serious."

We decided that while they were used to working under a boat, the mud and mire that was in the hole would be so thick they wouldn't be able to get a welder to work. But those Seals were ready to go.

People ask why we didn't let the Navy divers go in at the mine entrance. The divers thought they could get through, in spite of the fact that they would have to go a mile and a half through all kinds of debris and pitch blackness. But they weren't sure they could get back out. And besides, once they reached the miners, what would they do?

We just weren't willing to risk any more lives.

The determination of the Navy Seals is one of many examples of how people were willing to sacrifice to get this rescue done. Miners who worked at other mines would finish their shifts, then come to the rescue site and work. Mining companies offered so much equipment that some had to be turned away.

Meanwhile, during all the frustration of the drill bit breaking and unsuccessful attempts to free the broken bit from Rescue One, there was never any thought of giving up. We were going to see this through, and when hands weren't busy working on some aspect of the rescue, minds were occupied with possible solutions.

And then, the drill bit broke in Rescue Two.

As if to reflect the mood, thunder rumbled, and rain began to fall.

Depth = 160'
D.T.C. = 122'
40' casing
50 gpm
Sperry drilling 5-02

15A

14A

14B

14

2054.1

Depth = 150'
D.T.C. = 90'

Escape Well

6

14C

100

SP 30

Depth = 140'
D.T.C. = 100'

100A

WE

23M

2069.2

2098.0

23H

Depth = 230'
D.T.C. = 90'

Rescue #1

18

SP11

2073.5

23F

23G

SP180

23B

23E

23A

23C

23D

WE

NO MINING

2076.8

Depth = 135'
D.T.C. = 115'

1820

Depth = 16?'

CHAPTER SEVEN

BLESSING IN DISGUISE

When the second drill bit broke at 150 feet, I was at my lowest point. I couldn't help thinking, "Come on, God. Everything we try to do, you stop us. Give us a little help."

It was the lowest point of despair and frustration, and we knew our only option was to retrieve the broken bit out of Rescue One. I saw Brandon Fisher from Center Rock Drill Service standing at the bottom of the hill, talking on his cell phone and looking frustrated.

I said, "Brandon, what do you need?"

"Where's the closest fax machine?" he asked.

"My house."

I gave him the number, and he went to Yost and asked him who the manufacturer of the drill bit was. Brandon called the manufacturer and had the blueprints for the drill bit faxed to my house. From that blueprint, he got the measurements he needed to produce the overshot that would extract the drill bit.

Picture the broken drill bit as a water bottle with threads at the top for the lid. Brandon designed the perfect lid to fit on that bottle. He faxed the blueprints for the overshot to a Big Run company near Punxsutawney,

PA. Star Iron Works is the manufacturer of mining supplies like casings and overshots. When Brandon called Star Iron Works, he asked owner Frank Stockdale how long it would take to make the overshot.

The reply was, "Two and a half days."

Brandon said, "We don't have two and a half days."

Stockdale closed everything down, called in all of his employees, and told them the situation. They went to work building the overshot and cutting the threads to match those on the drill bit. Two men welded at the same time, and the 24-hour process of heat-treating the threads was skipped entirely.

In three hours, an Army National Guard helicopter landed in our field with a "very warm" overshot. It was so hot they had to cover it with a blanket and wear gloves to handle it.

The crane hooked onto the overshot and lowered it into the drill shaft. John Hamilton of Yost's Drilling was the operator attempting to hook onto the drill bit. He was working blindly—he had to go by feel as he attempted to turn the overshot into place.

The first attempt failed. Hamilton looked up, saw Mark Popernack's wife and sons watching him, and knew he couldn't disappoint them. When he made a second attempt around 4:00 p.m., he felt the overshot slide into place. He had it hooked, and gestured to the crane operator to bring it up.

FRIDAY 2002-07-25 4:00 P.M.
43 HOURS 15 MINUTES
TRAPPED UNDERGROUND

Once the 2,000-pound drill bit was out of the hole, it took five men to pull it out of the way. Then it was time to install a new drill bit and start the drilling. Although we were still less than halfway to our goal, excitement and relief filled the valley—we were back in business.

The only potential glitch was the fact that they were unable to find another 30-inch bit. There was a 26-inch bit available, and they decided to go with it, even though that meant the hole would be tighter for the 22-inch diameter cage. With the original bit, there would have been four inches of clearance between the cage and the shaft wall. Now, there would only be two inches clearance.

Another concern about going from a 30-inch to a 26-inch hole was that there would be a lip at the 105-foot point where the changeover occurred. That lip could catch the nine-foot-high capsule. There were no other options, however, so it was a risk we had to take.

Looking back on the rescue, we can see God's timing and all-knowing power. He knew that we had to have the sixteen-hour delay created by the broken bit.

While we were held up here, not doing any drilling, there were people in the cornfield down the road, at two other spots along Route 985, and at the mine entrance who were pumping water.

Some of the seals said if we would have entered the mine at the rate we were going with the 30-inch drill bit, we would have entered the mine at exactly the same time that the water had risen to its highest point. As a result, the mine could have decompressed so rapidly the men would have been killed—not by drowning but by being crushed to death by the weight of the water.

It would be like taking a jar and turning it upside down in a tub of water. The water only goes part way up the jar because of the air pressure inside the jar. The men were in a jar that happened to be 70 feet wide and 240 feet down. Out of 8,000 feet—a mile and a half from the mine entry—they were down to their last 70 feet of dry ground, but the 70-foot jar was keeping them safe. If we had broken through into the mine before the water level was pumped down, it would have been like taking a hammer and breaking the jar.

As the water level began to drop, slowly at first, but eventually at a rate of about a foot per hour, they kept pumping until they knew the water level was below the point where the rescue shaft was going to break through.

As the water was pumped out very slowly, very gradually, the men were also being decompressed very slowly, very gradually. In looking back on it, you could say the drill bit breaking was one of the many miracles that saved the miners' lives.

Because of the change in the size of the drill bit, and because it was vital that they achieve a perfectly straight hole, the operators decided to go slowly—only six inches an hour. They could have gone much faster, but they knew that if they were off by an eighth of an inch at the top, they would be off by 10 feet at the bottom, and the cage would have never gone down. At this point, accuracy was more important than speed. We drilled to within 13 feet of the mine, and then stopped the drilling to allow the water level to drop below the elevation of the air and rescue shafts.

We hadn't heard from the miners since Thursday morning, and this was late Saturday night, so as it was getting down to zero hour of breaking through, we were preparing for every possibility: live miners, injured miners, or dead miners.

By this time, the federal government was set up here. They were "in charge" and were starting to get testy about who was at the drill site. Some of the big head honchos were talking about what was going to happen next, and I walked up and stuck my head in this circle of guys. One fellow looked at me and not knowing who I was, right away called two or three people over and said, "Okay, we're going to put yellow ribbons on everyone's belt loops. Anyone who doesn't have a yellow ribbon on isn't allowed in the rescue zone."

So, everyone started putting on yellow police tape. There was police tape hanging everywhere, and I could have easily grabbed a piece of police tape and stuck it on my belt, but I didn't feel it was my place. I was standing back watching things develop, when Don Eppley of DEP's Mine Safety walked by.

I called him over and said, "Don, everyone's putting these yellow ribbons on. I don't want to be a jerk about this, but I started this thing, and I don't want to be thrown out now. I want to see it through to the end."

Don looked at me, half in disbelief that I would think I wouldn't be allowed inside the rescue zone, and half because he knew he was probably overstepping the bounds of protocol. But in the past three and a half days, we had gotten to work very closely with each other and had become comfortable with each other's abilities.

He said, "Are you kidding me? You're on my team. Come with me."

He reached past me, ripped a piece of yellow tape off, and said, "Here, get this on your belt."

I was on the team that would be the human shield in case the miners were incapacitated. There were men standing by for every contingency. If the miners were dead, there was an individual who was to go down into the mine and start the recovery. If the miners were injured, there was another person who was scheduled to be the first person into the mine to do triage, package the miners up, and get them into the capsule.

We didn't know which man was going to be the first one down, or if the miners were going to be able to get in the capsule on their own. Every option was scheduled and rehearsed.

One possibility was that the miners would be incapacitated—either injured or dead. The code word was "Shield." If we heard that word, there were about six of us who were supposed to go up and stand shoulder-to-shoulder to block people's view of an incapacitated miner.

While we discussed the procedure, Don looked around at his team of DEP guys who had gone through this several times in training and said, "Does anyone have a problem seeing a dead body?"

And when he said that, he looked directly at me. I knew what he was asking: if you're in a situation where you're going to see a dead person, are you going to be able to hold it together? Every part of me wanted to answer him, "YES, I do have a problem seeing a dead body come out of this hole. We didn't work this hard to get dead guys out. We're getting nine live guys out."

But I knew that wasn't what he was asking. He had to know if I could handle it because of professionalism and because it was what we might have to do. I felt my jaw tighten, and I nodded.

One of the other things we were going to be doing was man-handling the cable down into the shaft so it didn't become entangled, cut, or hung up while it was going down in or coming back up. There were six to eight of us handing the cable hand-over-hand to maintain a perfect, unkinked cable as it was going down into the rescue shaft. Everyone knew his job. We were all in place, and when the drill bit finally broke through into the mine, we were ready.

SATURDAY 2002-07-26 1:50 A.M.
53 HOURS 5 MINUTES
TRAPPED UNDERGROUND

CHAPTER EIGHT

BREAKTHROUGH

Once they punched through, we shut down all the air compressors for the first time in about four days. The miners were in the Number One entry in the highest part of the mine, and they could hear the compressors and drill rig running, but they didn't know that we had broken through because they had tried to barricade themselves from the water with a block wall around the 6-inch air shaft. It was only 20 feet from the rescue shaft, but in between the two shafts was a cement block wall.

When we shut everything down, it got deathly quiet in the mine, and the guys started to wonder if we had given up on them. Ron Hileman and Tom Foy came down from the Number One entry and started pounding on the 6-inch drill steel again. We heard their pounding, so we knew there were still men alive down there. The next thing we wanted to do was get communications down to them, so we pulled the 6-inch bit up. The miners said they were down there pounding away when the drill disappeared into the roof! They were angry, but in the stillness of the mine, they heard air whistling from the rescue shaft on the other side of the cement block wall.

Ron Hileman took Foy's hammer and broke one of the blocks out of the wall. When he saw the hole, he said, "They're in the mine, Tuck. We're goin' home."

He left Foy there to tear the rest of the wall down while he went back up to the Number 1 entry. Hileman stuck his head through the canvas the men had hung across the entry and said, "Who wants to go home?" This energized the exhausted miners, and they raced back to the hole.

[26-inch drill and bit used to complete the Rescue One shaft, now on display at the Visitor Center. Photo courtesy of Bill Arnold.]

Rob Zaremski of the Targeting Customer Safety firm had been called in to attempt communication with the miners. His equipment was a pen-shaped, two-way communications probe—the CON-SPACE Rescue Probe. It consisted of a speaker and a microphone inside a stainless steel compartment.

Zaremski had been stationed across the road at our farm pond listening for footsteps, thinking that perhaps the men had been able to find refuge in the old mine. He was happy to get out of there. For two days, he had been pestered by 40 two-month-old calves curious about the crazy man listening to the ground in their pasture.

Armed with his headset and 240 feet of cable, he attached a glow stick to his microphone so the miners could see it in the dark. The cable was fed over the shoulders of five men, and as the sensitive piece of equipment dropped down in the hole, Zaremski said over and over, "Can you hear me now?" He just kept talking. "What about a burger?" You guys must be starving."

John Phillippi and Ron Hileman saw the microphone and let out a yell. Like the other rescuers, Zaremski was very tired, but suddenly he snapped to attention. We knew he had heard something, but his next question seemed a bit neurotic: "Are you the nine miners that are trapped?"

Rob's taken a lot of ribbing because of that question. I was standing next to him, and I thought, "Who else does he think would be down there—the seven dwarfs?"

He told me later, "The reason I asked that question was my equipment was so sensitive that I was hearing state troopers out on the road. I was hearing helicopter guys back there in the landing zone. I was hearing firefighters on their walkie-talkies. I wanted to make sure I was talking to the miners and not to someone on a walkie-talkie."

That made perfect sense, but the guys in the mine thought the same thing I did when they heard the question. John Unger turned to the others and said, "Boys, we don't stand a chance—they don't even know who they're looking for."

The miners answered in the affirmative anyway, and Rob asked, "How many are you?"

They answered, "We're all nine here."

Rob looked at me, and if you remember seeing it broadcast on the news, he held up nine fingers. I was the person he was looking at when he did that. With my faith in the survival of the nine confirmed at last, I felt a huge burden come off my chest.

Then, John Phillippi had a question for Zaremsky: "What took you guys so long?"

Rescuers informed the miners they would be sending the capsule down and could send supplies down to them.

"What do you need?"

The miners didn't have to think long.

"Snuff!"

"Booze!"

After more than three days underground, it seemed like a strange request, but these were hardened miners doing a tough job in miserable conditions, and yes, they enjoyed their tobacco. The booze was requested by John Unger, who doesn't even drink. He explained later that he thought if he had a few shots of booze, he would just pass out and wake up outside the mine.

[The rescue capsule, now a familiar image across America, belongs to MSHA but is currently housed at the Quecreek Mine Rescue Foundation Educational Visitors Center. It is still on "active duty" should the need arise. Photo courtesy of Commonwealth Media Service]

Rescuers consulted the Navy medical team who said the alcohol wouldn't be advisable, but certainly give them their chew. Some of these men had been tobacco users for 32 years. Imagine the nicotine withdrawal they were going through.

So we prepared the capsule and put in it cap lights and candy bars, blankets and flashlights. Guys were pulling cans of snuff out of their pockets and throwing them in the capsule.

The nine-foot-tall rescue capsule measures 22 inches in diameter and hardly looks big enough to hold a full grown man. The capsule was built after the 1972 Sunshine Silver Mine accident in Idaho, where a similar capsule was used to rescue miners. This capsule was built by Westinghouse at a cost of $50,000. It's smaller than the capsule used in Idaho and has a better design. For 30 years, the capsule waited, unused, but always certified ready to go. It was housed in Beckley, West Virginia, because officials thought if the capsule would be needed anywhere, it would be in West Virginia's coal country.

When the MSHA officials were called about the accident in Quecreek, they had the capsule brought to the site, just in case it was needed. Now it was serving the purpose it had long ago been created for.

The airlock we had built with such difficulty ended up not being needed. Air pressure readings at the top of the shaft showed there was no difference between the pressure in the mine and the air pressure on the surface. The rate of the water going down and the air being forced into the mine had been at just the right ratio to equalize the pressure.

One last concern was the lip at 105 feet where the size of the drill bit had changed. In addition to the supplies for the miners, a headset was placed inside the capsule so the men could communicate with the surface on their way up. A small camera was fastened to the bottom of the capsule so rescuers could watch the descent and see if the lip was going to be a problem. When they reached the 105-foot level, however, they couldn't even see the lip. The capsule went down smoothly. In fact, after the miners were up, they told the rescuers the capsule had never touched the sides of the shaft. Miraculously, the hole was perfectly centered.

[The capsule is suspended, ready to be lowered into the rescue shaft for the first time. Photo courtesy of Commonwealth Media Service.]

Randy Fogle was the first man out of the mine. He was the crew's foreman and didn't want to be first, but the others insisted. He was the biggest miner and was also complaining of chest pains. That qualified him to be number one.

The height of the coal seam was four feet. The door on the capsule came up thirty-six inches, so Fogle had to hunker down and scramble in the cage. The reason the biggest man had to go first was because he would need help getting in. The other miners sat down and shoved him with their feet until he was in, then slid the door down.

When he arrived on the surface, he was soaking wet because the shaft had passed through several aquifers. Raincoats were sent down on the capsule for the other miners to wear on the way up, but even so, John Unger later said it was the coldest water he had ever felt.

On the surface, Fogle looked around and couldn't believe the people who were cheering for his rescue. Rescuers helped Fogle out of the capsule and onto a stretcher. Sipesville firefighters and the medical team had rehearsed the transfer of the miners from the capsule to the treatment units. The trip up the hill had to be smooth because jostling can trigger heart rhythm problems in patients who are extremely cold. Two physicians from the medical response team took turns escorting the stretchers, and each miner was delivered to the decontamination unit without incident.

There was a blue tent set up on the hill we called a MASH tent. They stripped Fogle, cleaned him off with Dawn dish detergent, started an IV, and wrapped him in blankets. He was assessed by a physician and then loaded onto a helicopter that took him to Conemaugh Memorial Hospital. Once there, doctors discovered his chest pains were actually indigestion.

The last eight men ascended in order from the largest to the smallest. The second man up was Blaine Mayhugh at 6'1" and 200 pounds. He and each of the other men went through the same triage as Fogle, and six of the eight were taken to hospitals in ambulances. Tom Foy and John Unger were evacuated by helicopter.

After Mayhugh was brought up, Gene Yost went to the crane operator and said, "This hole could collapse at any minute, so make it quick."

Afterwards, Yost said that without a casing in the hole past the 20-foot surface casing, a stone could have broken loose from the wall and wedged the capsule.

"When the last guy came up, I was tickled to death," he said.

It only took fifteen minutes or less for each of the remaining miners to be brought up: Tom Foy, John Unger, John Phillippi, Ron Hileman, Dennis Hall, and Robert Pugh, Jr. The last man out at 2:45 a.m. was Mark Popernack. He was the smallest miner and able to get into the capsule without help. When he had been trapped on the other side of the raging flood of water, he didn't think he would survive. But he did. By the grace of God and with the concerted effort of hundreds of people, all nine miners were safely on the surface in an hour and forty-eight minutes.

[Pennsylvania State Representative Bob Bastian (green jacket) congratulates Governor Mark Schweiker (blue helmet) with the rescue capsule in the back. Photo courtesy of Commonwealth Media Service.]

I didn't feel a sense of "hip hip hooray" as each man emerged. The reaction of the rescuers wasn't a celebration. It was more of a calm, respectful ovation—a salute to the miners. We weren't high-fiving each other and jumping up and down and whooping it up and throwing our hats in the air. It was quiet. Certainly, we were all exhausted, but no one was feeling the exhaustion at this point. We were all running on adrenalin and energy and jubilation, but each time we saw the capsule starting to come out of the ground, it was almost like a military salute— only with applause.

SUNDAY 2002-07-27 2:45 A.M.
78 HOURS
TRAPPED UNDERGROUND

CHAPTER NINE

A NEW CHAPTER

SUNDAY 2002-07-27 2:45 A.M.
2 HOURS 15 MINUTES
ABOVE GROUND

S unday morning after the rescue, we were deserted. Every single state, federal, and local worker disappeared. And with good reason. They had all been up for three to four days and needed some rest.

I was the third person to arrive at the rescue site and the last person to leave. At about five a.m., I turned off all the lights and locked up the doors of my now-deserted buildings. I couldn't help wondering if the last 78 hours had been a dream. The casings sticking up out of the 30-inch rescue shaft and the 6-inch air shaft confirmed the reality of the incredible events we had just lived through. And now it was over.

Or so I thought.

I was totally unprepared for the aftermath of the rescue. From Thursday morning on, we'd had all kinds of security at the site—military, state troopers, local cops, fire police. Sunday morning, it was Dad and me. And we were trying to deal with 2,000 people who had come to see the rescue site. The road coming in to the farm was parked full of cars. The places where no car could be parked were elbow to elbow with people. It looked like the midway at the county fair. The people came to see where the rescue happened or to pick up a souvenir. Some wrote messages on the guardrail in magic marker.

We went from having all the help we ever needed to having none at all. They did send two state troopers out and the sergeant of the local barracks. But then, one of the troopers went down with heat exhaustion, and the other trooper had to get him in his patrol car and take him to the hospital. So then we were back to having only the sergeant here.

One of the men I came to respect very highly during the rescue was Don Eppley (Epp). He is one of the safety instructors with the DEP, but throughout the rescue, his official title was "Liaison between the Landowner and the State Department." Basically, he was the Major underneath General Neff. Anything that needed done, Neff would go to Epp and say, "I need this, this, and this done." Later, Neff would say, "Anything I asked Don to do, I could ask him and forget about it, because I knew it was going to get done."

Everything Epp did, he did with efficiency and urgency. At the same time, he knew how to make things happen so we would not trip over them later on. You didn't have to come back and redo anything, because Epp already did it, and he did it right the first time.

As I tried to make sense of the mayhem that was taking place on my farm, a pickup pulled in, and Epp got out. He wasn't wearing a DEP hat or shirt or anything to identify his position. He wore a tee shirt, a pair of shorts, brand new white socks, and a pair of sandals.

I said, "Epp, what are you doing here?"

He said, "I knew what you were in for today. I knew you were going to need some help."

He gave me phone numbers of people I could call to get help on a state level. He said, "If we have to, we'll call the governor."

Then he handed me his cell phone and said, "Here, use my cell phone. I've got some of these numbers programmed into it."

As we were deciding whom to call first, I looked down and saw blood oozing through his brand new socks and sandals.

"What's the matter with your feet?"

"Don't worry about it," he said. "I've got some blisters from those dang wet work boots. I couldn't get my feet back in the boots; that's why I had to put these sandals on."

Like everyone else who was here during the four-day rescue, Epp had endured wet boots and wet feet. Now, here he was with blood leaking through his socks and sandals and in pain from the blisters, but he came just because he knew what we would be facing after the rescue. That's a good guy, and I will always consider him a friend.

Within a few days, we were to have another surprise. A family friend, who also happens to be our attorney, stopped in to see Dad and me. Five to six hundred people were already here visiting the site, and we were up in the building enjoying a few moments alone.

Our friend finally got around to telling us the purpose of his visit.

"Billy, the president wants to know if he can use your barn to meet the miners and their families."

I was completely naive. "The president of what? The mine? The union?"

He laughed and said, "No, Billy. THE President—of the United States."

Dad and I looked at each other. Dad started to chuckle and shake his head, and I remember saying, "Man, how cool is that?"

The president's advance team and Secret Service got in touch with us soon afterwards. They wanted to empty out both of the large farm buildings. As we walked through the buildings, the guy in charge of the Secret Service would say, "I want that machine to stay. I want that machine to go."

And I'm just sort of following along and saying, "Yeah. Okay. We can do that."

Once as we were walking, the guy looked around and said, "I really don't like this farm."

I kind of took that personally and said, "Well, what don't you like about it?"

He realized he had offended me and said, "Please don't misunderstand. You have a beautiful farm. But I don't like the layout. It's too open. Too flat. Not enough big buildings. Someone could shoot a rocket from a mile away, and we'd never see it coming. I like tall buildings in cities. That's a confined space, and I can control that environment for the president's safety. I don't like big open spaces. It would take an army of Secret Service to secure this farm."

As preparations were made for the meeting with the president, the Advance Team asked me to go over the list of people who were invited to the meeting and see if they missed anyone.

I was going down over the list, and it suddenly occurred to me that Neff's name wasn't on the list. I called the guy back and said, "Where's Larry Neff? He's not on any of the lists."

The man said, "Who's Larry Neff?" I explained to him all that Neff had done. He said, "Man, I'm going to call this guy personally and invite him. In fact, I'm going to have him invited directly from the Oval Office, because this is a guy the president would want to meet."

I said, "That's great. He deserves the honor."

I left it like that. Mission accomplished. That was Thursday.

On Saturday, I was going over the updated list, and Neff's name still wasn't on it. I called the guy back and said, "Look, did you invite Larry Neff? He's still not on the list."

He said, "Yes, I did. But he declined to come."

I thought, "What in the world?" I couldn't imagine why he would not want to meet the president.

By Friday or Saturday of that week, the Secret Service called to tell us they moved the meeting with the president to Greentree, near Pittsburgh, and they would provide a bus to take us.

"You and your family need to be in the Casebeer [the Lutheran church next door] parking lot at 7 a.m. Monday. If you're one minute late, we're leaving without you."

I was still mulling over the absence of Neff's name on the guest list Sunday morning. There was a special service for the miners at the Casebeer Church, and I saw Neff there.

I said to him, "Larry, how come you're not going to meet the president tomorrow?"

He said, "Oh, I don't need to go."

"But you deserve to go," I protested.

He explained that a family friend had passed away on Friday, and the funeral was on Monday. He had not gone to the funeral home yet, because he wanted to come to this special Sunday morning service.

"Monday morning, the president's not going to look around and say, 'Wait a minute, Neff's not here.' No one is going to miss me at the president's speech. But I'm going to go to the funeral for that friend of our family, and they're going to remember that."

I just started to cry. I thought, "Here is a man with class. A man with his priorities so straight that he would decline shaking hands with the President of the United States because a friend of the family—not even a relative, but a friend—passed away, and it's more important to him to be at the funeral for that family." He made a choice, and I am sure he never regretted it.

CHAPTER TEN

A DOME OF PRAYER

I n the days and weeks after the rescue, a steady stream of cars drove by to see the place where the miracle at Quecreek Mine happened. Men from the mine would come up and sit in their cars just below our barn to protect the place. The rescue shaft was not filled in and covered until late October or early November, and these miners took shifts so there was someone here 24 hours a day to make sure people did not get too close to the shaft and get hurt.

About three weeks post-rescue, I was headed to the barn to begin the day's milking when a car slowed and pulled in my gravel driveway. I tried to ignore it as I had to work, but the driver rolled down his window and called out, "Excuse me!"

The man and his two teenage sons had driven to the site from Arizona. "Could we just pick up a few stones from your driveway to take back with us? The boys wanted something to show they had been here. If you say 'No,' I'll respect that."

With my consent, the boys jumped out and filled their pockets with gravel from my driveway before they drove off. I've had people stop and pick up grass clippings for the same reason. People wanted to touch the place that was touched by the hand of God. They wanted to have something they could hold to take with them. I knew at that point that

I had two options; I could either put a fence around the site to keep people at a safe distance, or I could embrace it.

As people continued to visit, a few of them would leave money as a donation. We had no intention of collecting money from the people we allowed to come. Ninety-nine percent of the people who would visit the site would understand, but there would always be that one percent who would misinterpret our motives in accepting donations. That is why we began the process to become a 501(c)3 non-profit foundation in September of 2002.

Mom, Dad, and I approached all of the people who were involved in heading up the rescue to see who would be interested in serving on the foundation board. We wanted to make sure we had a diverse group of people who would have some good quality input to contribute, people with great backgrounds and abilities. Serving along with Mom and me on the Executive Board were Larry Neff and Pastor Joseph Beer, along with 30 advisory members, people who just wanted to come in to help and keep us focused.

I always tell the tour operators to go to the Flight 93 site in Shanksville before coming here. That site is somber and respectful, as it should be. The Quecreek site is happy and joyful. The two memorial sites are so different, and yet they are very similar. At Shanksville, 40 people died who boarded a plane with no plans or preparation to stop a terrorist attack. But they stood up and said, "We're going to make a difference," and by doing what they could, they affected history. They kept their wits and, with the few resources they had, helped people on the ground. They weren't professional warriors. They weren't trained to do what they did. But they stood up and drew a line in the sand.

During the mine rescue, we had a lot of professional people here, but there were also hundreds of people who weren't trained to do what they were asked to do, and every one of them stood up, drew a line in the sand and said, "We're going to get this done, no matter what it takes."

This strength of character has become part of our Somerset County heritage. It is what has made us America's County®[6]

President George W. Bush inadvertently got the ball rolling on that title during our meeting at Greentree. During his speech, he repeatedly referred to the "Spirit of America." Then at one point, he looked at me and said, "You know, with Shanksville [referring to the crash of United Flight 93] and now this accident at Quecreek, Somerset County is rapidly becoming the sweetheart of my nation."

[43rd President George W. Bush with Dorcas and Melvin Arnold. Photo courtesy of Dormel Enterprises.]

His words impressed me, and I later repeated them to our family friend and attorney, who told someone else, who told someone else, and it eventually made its way to the Director of the Somerset County Chamber of Commerce. It went through some transformations finally to become America's County®.

We have had people sign our guest book from all over the world. Some of them stand out clearly in my mind. Like the Japanese man and

6 "America's County" is a registered trademark of the Somerset County Chamber of Commerce.

his family who visited in October following the rescue. He, his wife, and two teenage children walked around the green building we were then using as a visitor center, whispering to each other.

I approached him and said, "Sir, have you signed our guest book?"

"No, I haven't."

He spoke excellent English, but with a heavy Japanese accent.

I was curious and looked over his shoulder as he signed the book. After his name, he wrote "M.D." and "Tokyo, Japan."

As I chatted with him, I asked what brought him to America. "Are you here on business?"

He said, "No."

"Are you visiting family?"

"No," he said and pointed to the rescue site. "We came to see this."

I thought, "This can't be right."

"You came from Japan to see this?"

He said, "Yes. I am a doctor."

I nodded. "I saw that when you wrote your name."

He said, "I am so sorry. It take me so long to get all my patients to go see other doctors so I could bring my family and come to see this."

I was dumbfounded to think that he would come all the way from Japan to see this hole in the ground. I thought, "Surely, there was another reason for his trip."

"Have you been to the Flight 93 site?"

His face went blank. "The what?"

"The Flight 93 crash site."

He still looked lost. "What is that?"

I said, "Remember September 11 last year when the United States was attacked by terrorists?"

He said, "Oh my, yes. Everyone knows that."

"You remember that one of the planes crashed?"

"Yes."

"It crashed only a few miles from here."

He looked astonished and said, "Really? How do I get there from here? Your roads are so crazy!"

I drew him a map and explained the directions. As we chatted, I looked at him again and said, "Did you really come from Tokyo, Japan, just to see this place?"

He stood up a little straighter and stuck his chin out with pride. "Yes. We watch the whole thing on Tokyo CNN."

This is just one of dozens of stories I could tell about the people who have blessed us with their visit.

One thing we hear repeatedly from our guests is, "I wish I could have done more. All I could do was sit in front of my television and watch every minute." People were glued to their sets in Dallas, and Seattle, and

Wyoming, and around the world. They say to me, "All I could do was sit in front of my TV and pray."

I tell them, "That was enough."

We could feel it. We could feel the prayers of the nation like a dome of protection over the rescue site. And I want people reading these words today to know we could feel your prayers. More importantly, God heard them, and He answers prayer. Not always in a manner we understand or are willing to accept, but He always answers prayer.

CHAPTER ELEVEN

PRESERVING A RESCUE

Events moved rapidly the first year after the rescue. Even as we incorporated as a non-profit, changes were being made in the little pasture that had once been filled with drilling equipment. In October or early November, the rescue shaft was filled with concrete and capped for safety. And the people continued to come.

Offers came, too. People and businesses called and wanted to do things for the site. We were offered nine enormous crosses, but after some discussion with Mom and Dad, we felt they would be too overpowering in the small area. As we talked, Mom asked, "Why don't we plant trees?"

I said, "That's a great idea, Mom. And why don't we make them nine evergreen trees that never lose their lives?"

Dad said, "I'll do one better than that. I'll plant nine evergreen trees AND one red oak in the middle to represent God."

We agreed that was great, but I felt we would have to write something on a board so people would understand the symbolism.

The very next day, I was mixing feed for the cows and had an epiphany. I knew what I would paint on that board. I was struck by these words and I knew they were not coming from me, because I am not that smart. I wanted to write them down so I wouldn't forget them, but I did not have any paper. I grabbed a white Arm & Hammer™ feed sack and wrote the words on the back. Later, I transcribed them to a notebook, and for the moment, the feed sack was forgotten.

[Photo courtesy of Bill Arnold.]

The very next day, I got a call from the president of Matthews Bronze in Pittsburgh. I did not recognize the name, and he explained that they were the company that donated the bronze plaques for the World Trade Center, the Pentagon, and Flight 93.

"We'd like to donate a plaque to your rescue site. Do you have anything you'd like to have put on a plaque?"

I told him I thought I might have something. One week later, the plaque was delivered to our site, and we mounted it on a huge rock.

Mom let me know that she wanted that feed sack. I told her I did not think I had it anymore, but she insisted, "I want it." I looked through my stacks of sacks twice, but could not find it. Weeks later, I was stuffing empty feed sacks under a brush pile I was burning when I suddenly saw it, just moments before it would have been added to the fire.

At this point, just a few months after the rescue, I was still recovering

I took it to Mom and said, "Here's an early Christmas present."

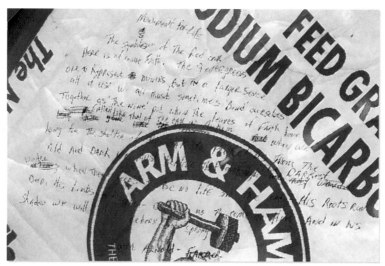

[A portion of the paper feedsack hanging in the visitor's center. Photo courtesy of Bill Arnold.]

She took it, had it framed, and gave it back to me around Christmas. It hangs in the Visitor's Center to this day. The plaque reads:

The symbol of the red oak, here, is of course, faith. The 9 evergreens are to represent miners, but in a larger sense, all of us. We all must sometimes bind ourselves together as "the nine" did when the leaves of faith have fallen like that of the oak in autumn. When we long for the shelter of the oak to protect us from the cold and dark, we must realize that in the coldest winter of our lives, or the darkest mine, when there seems to be no life in the oak—His roots run deep. His limbs outstretched—calling us to Him. And in His shadow, we will all be reborn in spring.

We had a lot to do to prepare for the first anniversary of the rescue. The trees were in place, the plaque was on the stone in the center, but there was a lot of landscaping and cleaning up to do. A monument company offered us nine granite stones for the Memorial Park. They delivered the stones the night before the anniversary, and we unloaded them by flashlight. They completed the symbolism of the Memorial Park; the nine evergreens represent the nine miners who were rescued. They encircle a majestic oak tree that symbolizes the faith and strength everyone showed in bringing the nine to safety, as well as the power of

God at work during those fateful 78 hours. In addition to the trees, nine black granite monuments also encircle the Red Oak to honor the first nine miners who narrowly escaped the mine flood, soon to become rescuers themselves.

[The Quecreek Mine Rescue Memorial as it looked shortly after completion. The covered rescue shaft and 6-inch air shaft are in the foreground, and the airlock built on-site is in the background. Photo courtesy of Joyann Dwire.]

We were also privileged, in July 2003, to unveil a seven-foot cast bronze coal miner in honor of coal miners everywhere. It was made by Alan Cottrill, a sculptor from Zanesville, Ohio.

Nearly all the miners came out for that first anniversary celebration, as well as many of the state and local dignitaries who were involved. We have been gratified each year at the support we continue to receive as we honor each anniversary.

At the Second Anniversary Celebration, we announced plans to move the Fire Hall from nearby Sipesville. The historic building had been a schoolhouse more than a century ago and then served the community as a fire hall. As word of the accident in the mine went out, officials directed families to the fire hall to wait for news. Pastors stayed with them and provided consolation while area restaurants, the Salvation Army, Red Cross and many volunteers prepared food and provided blankets and cots for the families and rescue workers. So many people were in the building that at one point officials were concerned the old floor was going to collapse.

It was late Saturday night when the governor conveyed the good news to the families waiting at the fire hall. Karen Popernack, step-mother of miner

[A lone miner reads Scripture from the Bible, as depicted by sculptor Alan Cottrill. Photo courtesy of Bill Arnold.]

[Mark Popernack's family anxiously waits. Photo courtesy of Commonwealth Media Service.]

Mark Popernack, recalls the governor's entrance and the anticipation the families felt as he made his way to the stage.

The governor got up on the stage, raised his arms, and made his announcement: "All nine are alive!"

The fire hall, for so long a place full of fear and despair, erupted with shouts of hope and tears of joy. The families watched the rescue on a television that was set up for them, and a mine representative told them which miner was in the rescue capsule before it emerged from the ground. Families were then informed which hospital their loved one had been taken to. By early Sunday morning, the fire hall was empty.

I like to affix a personality to the fire hall and imagine it had said, "I can do this. I'm up to the task." Just as every other rescuer did, it said, "I'm not sure how, but I will give my best to this rescue." Although this old building is very near and dear to all of our hearts, unfortunately, it had fulfilled its purpose and was deemed no longer structurally sound for public use.

The fire company had plans to build a new fire hall, and it was our desire to save the historic building and move it to the rescue site. It seemed like the move was a go; however because of the lack of structural integrity of the building, relocating it proved impossible. On the advice of the mover, the Quecreek Mine Rescue Foundation agreed to purchase several of the key components of the fire hall, including the pillars and stage, from the Sipesville Fire Department.

Another treasure we have been given the privilege to preserve is the original rescue capsule that traveled 240 feet into the earth and brought nine miners to safety. The rescue gave the capsule a bit of celebrity, and it has traveled extensively across the United States. When it was on display, two federal mining officials accompanied the capsule. For two years, it was still an active piece of rescue equipment and was available for any emergency. After a new rescue capsule was built, this historic artifact came "home." It was donated to the Quecreek Mine Rescue Foundation by the U.S. Department of Labor Mine Safety and Health Administration on October 14, 2004.

The dedication ceremony was attended by Penn State engineers, MSHA officials, state representatives, and Somerset County Commissioners. Among the comments made by Dave Lauriski, Assistant Secretary of Labor for Mine Safety and Health, were these words:

It seems only fitting that the bright yellow steel capsule that has become such a recognizable symbol of the Quecreek rescue should make its home here in Somerset.

The capsule is among the first things visitors notice when they walk into the visitor's center, and rightly so. As former Somerset County Commissioner Jimmy Marker said, "Anyone who remembers Quecreek remembers this capsule."

It will always have a place of honor in our visitor's center.

A few weeks after the rescue, a flag that was draped over the Pentagon after 9/11 was given to PBS Coals, the Somerset company who owned the property on which United Flight 93 crashed and also was connected to the Quecreek mining operation. After a ceremony at the Flight 93 National Memorial, PBS Coal representative John Weir, who was the

[A rare photo of all 18 miners, with volunteers, rescuers, and family at the dedication of the Pentagon flag. Photo courtesy of Dormel Enterprises.]

initial "point man" for communicating with the miners' families, brought the flag to the Quecreek rescue site, where it is proudly on display still today.

We are also pleased to have the replica capsule used in the 2002 Disney movie, *The Pennsylvania Miners' Story*. In 2014, we acquired a number of exhibits and artifacts from the Windber Coal Heritage Museum.

For the first seven years, Dad's green building, where rescuers were able to go for food and rest, served as the Visitor Center. In 2008, ground was broken just above the Monument for Life, and today that new center houses artifacts and memorabilia of mine history, as well as the rescue.

[Dormel Farms, photo courtesy of Bill Arnold.]

July, 2017 marked the 15th anniversary of the rescue. It is incredible to think that in the years since those 78 dramatic hours, we have continued to host an average of 5,000 visitors a year. Many of them are repeat visitors, bringing their friends and family with them to see the place where the miracle happened.

As long as they come, we will be here to meet them.

EPILOGUE
WHERE ARE THEY NOW?

SOMERSET COUNTY

Like the rest of the country, Somerset County has gone through an economic downturn. The population in 2002 was approximately 80,023. By 2016, the population had fallen to around 77,000. Factory closures and a lack of jobs have been major factors in that difference. At one time, coal mining and agriculture were the top industries in the county. Now, between the Flight 93 National Memorial, Seven Springs Mountain Resort, and the Quecreek Mine Rescue Museum, tourism is the main industry.

QUECREEK MINE

The Quecreek Mine was able to reopen in October 2002 and continues to operate as of this writing. The latest reports show they are close to running out of coal and will probably be forced to shut down some time before 2020.

DORMEL FARMS

Built in 1791 and listed on the Pennsylvania Historic Registry, Dormel Farms is still a working dairy farm, now certified organic, with over 150 head of dairy cattle as of this writing, 75 milking. The barn built in 1837 is still used every day.

THE MINERS

All but two of the rescued miners continue to live in Somerset County.

Mark Popernack works for the same coal company. However, he stays above ground.

John Unger worked a surface job for the coal mine until his retirement.

Robert Pugh and Tom Foy have retired. Neither returned to the coal mine.

John Phillippi works for the Turnpike Commission and lives in a neighboring county. His son is now working underground as a coal miner.

Blaine Mayhugh now works as an electrician for CSX Railway.

Neither **Ronald Hileman** nor **Dennis Hall** returned to the mine. Hileman lives in a neighboring county. Hall continues to live in Somerset County.

Perhaps the most interesting story belongs to crew chief and first man up, **Randy Fogle**. Six months after the accident, he returned to work in the mine and immediately went back underground. He has been promoted several times and is now Mine Superintendent, in charge of the entire mine operation.

[Several of the nine Quecreek Miners reunite on the 15th anniversary of their rescue. Top row left to right: Dennis "Harpo" Hall, Bob "Boogie" Pugh, Ron "Hound Dog" Hileman, Former Pennsylvania Governor Mark Schweiker, John "Ung" Unger. Bottom row left to right: Tom "Tucker" Foy, Bill Arnold (Author), John "Flathead" Phillippi, Joe Sbaffoni, DEP (retired) Photo courtesy of Megan Critchfield.]

We would be remiss if we failed to honor the first nine miners to make it out of the mine. They are:

Doug Custer	**Barry Carlson**
Wendell Horner	**Joe Kostyk**
Dave Petree	**Ryan Petree**
Ron Schad	**Frank Stewart**
Larry Summerville	

Thank you for your loyalty and commitment as you participated in the rescue.

NOTABLE WITNESSES

Former Pennsylvania Governor Mark Schweiker returned to private life the following year in 2003. He and his wife, Kathy, went on to raise three children in their native Bucks County. Governor Schweiker continues his professional life as an executive with a biochemical manufacturer headquartered in suburban Philadelphia.

Joe Sbaffoni retired as Director, PA Bureau of Mine Safety in June, 2015 with 30 years of Commonwealth Service and over 45 years in the mining industry. He presently runs a private consulting firm offering professional services to the mining industry. He says, *"The Quecreek mine rescue is the high point of my mining career and will always hold a special place in my heart. It was a massive effort that took place over four days and demonstrated sound engineering, surveying, drilling, pumping, great decision making and a never quit attitude by all involved. I am very proud to have played a part in bringing nine miners home to their loved ones."*

Larry Neff continues to work his 200-plus acre Pennsylvania farm with his wife Theresa, where he raises 120 head of Angus cattle. He also works with a private steel production and mining company as a water quality specialist.

David Hess is now a partner in a Harrisburg-based government affairs firm working on environmental issues.

[Wedding photo of Dorcas and Melvin Arnold. Photo courtesy of the Arnold family.]

Dorcas and Melvin Arnold, Bill's parents, married 63 years as of 2017, have been living in a nursing home since Thanksgiving of 2016. Bill says:

"Dad is suffering from 'Alzheimer's' and unable to live at home. Dad scarcely remembers the rescue, and sometimes, I fear, he is unsure of who I am. Some memories hold fast though. Recently my sister was going through old photos and came across one of Mom and Dad's wedding pictures, taken July 24th, 1954.

As she shuffled through, laying those on the table that she wanted to copy, Dad watched quietly. After my sister lay the wedding photo on the table, Dad leaned forward, touched the photo and said,"That's my girlfriend."

Bill Arnold continues to work his Certified Organic dairy farm, now with over 150 head of dairy cattle, and looks after his parents, Dorcas and Melvin Arnold, who live not far away. He encourages others who think of themselves as incapable of rising up to a challenge, should God call them to it. Bill says:

> *We don't realize how much we have been learning across our lifetime until we are called upon to use it. Like Captain "Sully" Sullenberger [famous for landing U.S. Airways Flight 2549 safely on the Hudson River in 2009] said in his interview with Katie Couric shortly after the incident: "One way of looking at this might be that for 42 years, I've been making small, regular deposits in this bank of experience, education and training. And on January 15, the balance was sufficient so that I could make a very large withdrawal."*

> *The Quecreek accident required all of us to "make withdrawals" from our banks of experience. And, all would agree, no experience would have been enough had not God Himself intervened over and over again. On top of all of the details only God could have arranged, He took ordinary men and women and made them extraordinary just when they needed to be.*

In addition to his farming, Bill also manages and conducts tours at the museum, is an inspirational speaker, and is called upon to comment by major news networks around the world whenever a mining disaster occurs, including the Chilean mining accident of 2010.

On one such occasion, the reporter asked one final question: "What do you have to say to the families waiting for word?"

Bill replied,

"Hold on to hope for as long as possible,
and as hope fails, cling to faith.
Because miracles do still happen."

A MESSAGE FROM BILL ARNOLD

I mentioned in previous chapters how my life has changed since the rescue. There is one more change I never expected. Sadly, my wife, who experienced all of these things alongside me, is no longer a part of my life, after twenty years together. This book has become part of my healing process. As many others have found, going through a divorce is life altering.

I write this as a cautionary tale to all married men. There are evil forces in this world, and they will try to steal both your family and your marriage. If you believe it could not happen to you, it can. I am living proof of that.

No matter how strong you think your marriage is, no matter how committed you are to your family, you need to be ever vigilant in looking out for your relationships. First, in your relationship with your creator. Second, in being comfortable in your own skin and in your relationship with your spouse and children. Someone has said there is no stasis in any relationship: either you are growing closer or you are going farther apart. There is no even keel.

So, my family life has changed. My farming operation has changed. The operation of the visitor center has changed. Most of all, I have changed.

You have to find a way to move forward. This is true no matter what trauma or crisis you face. I have not done that well. In fact, I have been dragged along kicking and screaming.

Let me end on an encouraging note. One Bible verse that has meant a lot to me and has helped to carry me through talks about waiting on the Lord. We do not like to wait. We hated it as children, and we continue to hate it as adults. But when you are waiting on the Lord, the result will always be amazing. You will mount up on wings like eagles.

> *"But those who wait on the Lord Shall renew their strength;*
> *they shall mount up with wings like eagles, they shall run and not*
> *be weary, they shall walk and not faint."*
> *—Isaiah 40:31 (NKJV)*

[Photo courtesy of Harrison Buss]

ABOUT THE AUTHOR

Bill Arnold is Executive Director of the Quecreek Mine Rescue Foundation, an internationally known inspirational speaker, and an international media consultant on the subject of mining disasters.

Ten months after 9/11, when United Flight 93 flew over his farm just seconds before crashing into a field a few miles away, Bill found himself literally one of the first to arrive at the scene of a second disaster as nine Quecreek miners became trapped by floodwaters from an abandoned mine situated below his property.

As the men fought for their lives 240 feet below Dormel Farms, his family's historic 200-year-old home and dairy cow business, Bill joined the rescue effort, volunteering his aging farm equipment to assist and actually "turning the first earth" in the now world-renowned *Miracle at Quecreek Mine*. His tireless efforts throughout the 78-hour drama put him in the spotlight as international media converged on the county once again. He has appeared on every major news network, including the *Today Show*, *Good Morning America*, *Fox and Friends*, CNN, BBC, *Larry King Live*, and *Geraldo*.

Bill has been a media consultant for nearly every mine rescue since 2002, including the successful rescue of the 33 Chilean Miners in South America in 2010. He was invited to the Smithsonian Institute in Washington, D.C. by Chilean President Sebastián Piñera for the opening of the Chilean Mine Rescue exhibit.

In the years since this historic rescue, Bill has written two books about the event. Bill has started a non-profit foundation to "preserve the site and celebrate the inspirational story of the Quecreek Mine Rescue."

Bill continues to run Dormel Farms in Somerset, now a Certified Organic Dairy Farm with over 150 head of cattle, and still greets over one hundred motor coaches and over 5,000 guests per year that come to experience the events that took place on his historic property.

ABOUT THE QUECREEK MINE RESCUE FOUNDATION

Mission Statement: To preserve the site, and celebrate the inspirational story of the Quecreek Mine Rescue.

The Quecreek Mine Rescue Memorial and Monument for Life honors and portrays the team of rescue workers who saved nine trapped coal miners from certain death near Somerset, Pennsylvania. In a larger sense, the memorial site honors the tireless heroism of rescue workers everywhere, as well as serving as a lasting tribute to the coal miners of Southwestern Pennsylvania and across the nation.

The successful rescue of the nine miners drew international attention and emotion from July 24 to 28, 2002. The catastrophe and ensuing rescue captured the hearts and hopes of millions of people worldwide. Since the rescue on July 28, tens of thousands of people from around the world have visited the farm to view the site where the miners were rescued.

The Monument for Life will be the largest permanent tribute to America's rescue workers in the United States. To learn how you can make a tax deductible contribution to the Quecreek Mine Rescue Foundation to support the Monument for Life visit our website: http://www.quecreekrescue.org/donate.php .

QUECREEK MINE RESCUE FOUNDATION EDUCATIONAL VISITORS CENTER INFORMATION

Address:
140 Haupt Road
Somerset, PA 15501

Phone:
814-445-5090

Hours:
Open Tuesday through Saturday 11a.m. to 4p.m. If you plan on visiting on the weekend, please schedule in advance.

Admission:
$7.00 per person to tour the Visitors' Center and Monument for Life grounds.

Last tour:
Starts before 3:15 p.m. Be sure to plan accordingly. You can expect the tour and the presentation to last at least one hour.

Tip: Please check the Bus Tour page to see if we have anything scheduled for the day of your visit. Joining in with a bus tour is the best way to hear the story. If you want to sit in with a tour, please call ahead so we can prepare for you and confirm the expected presentation time. *http://www.quecreekrescue.org/info.php*

Directions from Interstate 70/76: From Interstate 70/76 (PA Turnpike) take exit 110 toward US 219/Somerset/Johnstown. Turn onto PA-601 North and follow it 3.6 miles. PA-601 will then become

PA-985. Follow PA-985 north for .86 miles. The memorial site is on the left. Watch for the sign.

Directions from the Flight 93 Memorial: Take Route 30 West to Jennerstown, then Route 985 South for 6 miles.

For more information, to order more copies of this book, or to make a donation, visit our website at www.quecreekrescue.org, or call or write:

Quecreek Mine Rescue Foundation
140 Haupt Road
Somerset, PA 15501
Phone: 814-445-5090

ORDER THE BOOK
CONTACT THE AUTHOR

Miracle at Quecreek Mine is available at the museum and locally in Somerset County. It is also available on line, through the publisher, or may be ordered through your favorite bookstore:

ISBN # 9780998559247

Published by Encourage Publishing
www.shop.encouragebooks.com
812-987-6148

Bill Arnold is available for speaking engagements and may be contacted through the publisher or at:

www.BillArnoldSpeaks.com